Matthew Lloyd

# How the Movie Brats Took Over Edinburgh

## The Impact of Cinéphilia on the
## Edinburgh International Film Festival, 1968-1980

**St Andrews Film Studies**
**2011**

First published in Great Britain in 2011 by St Andrews Film Studies
99 North Street, St Andrews, KY16 9AD, Scotland, United Kingdom
Secure on-line ordering: http://www.st-andrews.ac.uk/filmbooks
Publisher: Dina Iordanova



British Library Cataloguing-in-Publication Data
A catalogue record for this book is available from the British Library.

ISBN 978-0-9563730-2-1 (paperback)

The book is published with the assistance of the
Centre for Film Studies at the University of St Andrews
and the Carnegie Trust for the Universities of Scotland.
St Andrews Film Studies promotes greater understanding
of, and access to, international cinema and film culture
worldwide.

The University of St Andrews is a charity registered in
Scotland, No. SC013532

Front cover design: Matthew Lloyd and Duncan Stewart, based on the
transcript held by the National Library of Scotland of an interview conducted
with Samuel Fuller in 1986 as part of an unidentified TV documentary about
the Edinburgh Film Festival.

Cover and pre-press: University of St Andrews Print & Design

Printed and bound in the UK by MPG Books Group, Bodmin and King's Lynn

# Contents

# Acknowledgments

My foremost thanks to the former staff of the Edinburgh International
Film Festival who were so generous with their time and memories:
Murray Grigor, Lynda Myles and David Will. My thanks also to Mark
Cousins, for introducing me to Murray and Lynda, and to Sally Harrower
at the National Library of Scotland, for her friendly advice. Adam Budd
set me on the path, Melanie Selfe and Lynne Stanford kindly allowed
me to view unpublished drafts of their work and Kim Knowles and
Dorota Ostrowska gave guidance and reassurance at critical stages. My
thanks to Martine Beugnet for her patience; to Dina Iordanova, Lars
Kristensen, George Nalbantov, Alex Marlow-Mann and Duncan Stewart
for bringing this work to publication; and finally to Emily Munro for her
unstinting encouragement, her tenacious pursuit of flabby writing and her
unconditional love.

# A Note on Referencing

Because of the unsystematic nature of the Edinburgh International Film
Festival (EIFF) collection at the National Library of Scotland (NLS), in the
bibliography I have chosen to follow my predecessor Lynne Stanford in
referencing documents from the archive as follows: the term 'Acc' refers to
the accession number of the EIFF collection at the NLS and MS refers to the
folder number containing the cited manuscript.

As I cite unpublished interviews throughout this book – both the
transcripts of interviews conducted by anonymous interviewers in 1986
which are held in the EIFF collection and those that I conducted myself
in 2008 – I have chosen to cite these sources as 'Interview'. A list of these
interviews can be found at the end of the bibliography; in the case of the
EIFF transcripts, which lack clearly distinguishing references or page
numbers, the bibliography also cites the Acc and MS.

# Preface

In June 2008 I left the staff of the Edinburgh International Film Festival (EIFF). Having worked for EIFF in various capacities for 10 editions, under three successive Artistic Directors, I'd witnessed what I felt was a period in which the organisation experienced increasing uncertainty concerning its own identity. My first EIFF took place in August 1999, when the supposedly unfashionable aesthetic of Robert Bresson, the subject of that year's retrospective, was repeatedly echoed in new films by young directors. Successive years saw great films and events, but no comparable critical focus. However, during this period attendance figures rose exponentially, significant partnerships with major sponsors were formed and in 2008 the UK Film Council awarded the Festival an unprecedented £1.88 million of Lottery funding over three years. What did this mean for the Festival? Was it still, as John Huston remarked in 1972, 'the only festival worth a damn' (quoted in F. Hardy 1992: 112), or had it become a festival 'like all the others' (McArthur 1990: 101)?

That same summer, I attended the world's oldest film festival, Venice, and its youngest at the time, The Ballerina Ballroom Cinema of Dreams, in Nairn, North-East Scotland. At Venice I witnessed the rituals that exemplify the 'festival experience' – glamorous red carpet photo-calls, snaking colour-coded queues, lengthy introductions of cast and crew before screenings. With its Fascistic stage-managed splendour, there was a strong sense that the event had barely changed since its inception.

The Nairn event, co-directed by former EIFF Director Mark Cousins and actress Tilda Swinton, was remarkable not only for its deviation from this notion of a film festival, but also for the fact that, under the surface, it shared certain key characteristics. Whilst Venice is an exclusive event based on segregation, Nairn was inclusive, with entrance costing a mere £3 or a tray of home baking. Venice premieres new work by established world auteurs; Nairn screened an eclectic mix of classic and neglected films from DVD. A large proportion of Venice attendees are press and industry delegates, pursuing their own agendas; the Nairn audience, whether locals or long-distance visitors, came for the love of cinema, creating a shared sense of community. Whilst Venice maintains clearly recognised rituals year upon year, Nairn thrived on makeshift improvisation during its self-proclaimed '*Brigadoon*-like' brief lifespan.

Yet Nairn also created rituals around each screening – the playing of a song, a spotlight drifting over the audience, Swinton and Cousins holding a flag in front of the screen proclaiming us to be in the 'State of Cinema'. Despite its self-consciously down-at-heel inclusiveness, Nairn also traded on star glamour. Without an Oscar-winning actress at the helm, would this one-off event based in a small town in the far North of Scotland have secured over £10,000 of state funding, or garnered press coverage in trade journals and the international media, or attracted sell-out crowds to screenings of 15 year-old Senegalese or Iranian films? These similarities begged the question of whether a festival that specifically defines itself in opposition to traditional notions of a film festival can continue to operate in a highly competitive market.

This question led me to back to Edinburgh and to a time when, it has been suggested, EIFF became 'a unique rallying point for progressive forces in British culture' (Willemen 1980: 2). Between 1969 and 1980 the Festival pursued a policy of expressly opposing dominant modes of film consumption. In examining this period within its cultural context, I aimed to discover how it came about and whether it was inevitably a short-lived anomaly in the Festival's history.

The UK Film Council's grant to EIFF has now come to an end. Indeed under the new austerity of the coalition government the UKFC itself is to cease operations by 2012. As government arts budgets are slashed and private sector funders become scarce, EIFF has to reconsider its priorities and identity in the face of a significant reduction in funding. Could EIFF of the 1970s offer a clue as to how the Festival in its present state could be reinvigorated for the future?

# Introduction

In May 1968, a group of young filmmakers led by the Nouvelle Vague
directors Jean-Luc Godard and François Truffaut brought the Cannes
Film Festival to a premature halt. They declared their action to be a show
of solidarity with the Parisian workers and students protesting against
President Charles de Gaulle's centralised, culturally stifling rule. Over the
subsequent four years Cannes reorganised itself, replacing a programme
of national cinemas with that of individual auteurs and giving space
to quasi-independent sidebar events curated by filmmakers or critics.
These reforms were consolidated in 1972 when the Festival Director was
given responsibility for programme selection, which had previously been
controlled by national committees that submitted a selection of their annual
output (Corless et al. 2007: 149).

Thomas Elsaesser states that with this 'crucial change [...] Cannes set the
template for film festivals the world over' (2005a: 90). By charting the
development of the Edinburgh International Film Festival (EIFF)[1] in the
decade following May '68 I intend to question this statement, arguing that
in order to understand the changes that took place in film festivals during
the period, one must assess both the internal workings of each organisation
and the wider culture. In the case of Edinburgh, I will illustrate how
the Festival negotiated three interlinked factors – its own reputation,
the politicisation of cinéphilia and the emergence of 'film study culture'
(Munro 2006: 110) – in order to re-assert the identity it had once enjoyed as
a unique and vital film event.

Recent research on the subject of the film festival circuit identifies it as an
alternative distribution network – a global economy, both at odds with
and complementary to Hollywood (Stringer 2001; Elsaesser 2005a). Julian
Stringer describes festivals as playing 'a key, if often under-acknowledged,
role in the writing of film history. Festival screenings determine which

movies are distributed in distinct cultural arenas, and hence which movies critics and academics are likely to gain access to' (2001: 135). Marijke de Valck argues that film festivals have become 'so important to the production, distribution, and consumption of many films that, without them, an entire network of practices, places, people, etc. would fall apart' (2007: 36). Therefore film festivals both map and construct the discourses and trends surrounding film production, distribution and consumption, or 'film culture'.

The consequences of May '68 are significant for international film culture in several interrelated ways. Young British and American intellectuals in the first flushes of the push to have film studies taken seriously as an academic discipline adopted French theoretical ideas with a militancy previously unseen in academic institutions. Cannes, and the events of the 'Langlois Affair' of February that year, marked a new politicisation of the cinéphilia that had previously been promoted in various forms by journals *Cahiers du cinéma, Positif* and *Présence du cinéma* and been lived out by the front row audience at Henri Langlois' Cinémathèque Française. The Cannes disruption and similar protests at other 'A-list' festivals exposed their conflicting agendas and lack of engagement with new film movements, thereby legitimising young, independent festivals modelled on thematic lines.

De Valck calls the post-'68 period 'the age of the programmers' (2007: 168) and suggests that it constituted a necessary revolt against the dominance of geopolitical agendas in which politicised film cultural concerns were foregrounded, regardless of market constraints or demands:

> Never before had [festival programmers] had so much freedom to pursue their cinéphile and critical agendas without being restrained by national politics or economic interests, never again would programming be as pure and unaffected by audience

expectations or the financial side of event management that would eventually become increasingly important during the 1980s. (De Valck 2007: 168)

The question arises, therefore, of what impact the festival circuit of the 1970s had on film culture; did it merely constitute an inevitably short-lived and utopian period in film festival development? This problem is at the centre of my study of EIFF during this period.

The post-'68 period saw EIFF's international reputation grow as its critical approach to film culture became more focused. This was a period in which increasing professionalism was balanced by the independence afforded by financial paucity, a time in which the Festival was prepared to question traditional notions of a film festival's role. Whilst this study also refers to other festivals in order to place Edinburgh in an international context, concentrating on this particular event is important for two reasons. Firstly, although during the 1970s EIFF was arguably one of the most significant festivals in the world and the inspiration and model for such a contemporary giant as Toronto (Myles 1977a), the Festival has been largely ignored by the critical discourse on the international film festival phenomenon. Secondly, EIFF is the oldest continually running festival in the world, having never once cancelled an edition since its inception in 1947. In an increasingly competitive market this is no mean feat for a festival which throughout its 64 years has never enjoyed the level of financial support or official recognition of its near contemporaries, Cannes and Venice, both of which have at times been forced to roll up the red carpet (Corless et al. 2007: 231). Arguably, therefore, EIFF has proved itself highly adept at responding to changes in film culture. The aims of this study are to determine how an organisation such as EIFF reinvents itself, and to consider whether by deviating from traditional concepts of the film festival as showcase or marketplace, the Festival was in danger during the 1970s of isolating itself from the wider culture.

By concentrating predominantly on the period between May 1968 and the 1980 edition of EIFF, this study focuses on the work of two successive cinéphile artistic directors, Murray Grigor (1967-72) and Lynda Myles (1973-80),[2] during which time the Festival pursued a specific policy of intervention into film culture (Will, Interview). The end of Myles' term of office marks a transition for the Festival determined less by the agenda of the incoming director, Jim Hickey, than by financial concerns and wider shifts in film culture.[3]

This study takes the form of a historical account, placing EIFF's own history within that of the post-war international film festival phenomenon, the rise of cinéphilia in the 1950s and 1960s, and the emergence of film study culture following May '68. It begins with a brief review of the theoretical writing on the film festival phenomenon; whilst such work is useful in gaining an understanding of the operations of the festival circuit, I will suggest that it is of limited value in defining Edinburgh's unique identity, particularly during a period in which EIFF explicitly stood outside traditional notions of what a film festival should deliver.[4]

# Context and Method

Although film festivals have generated a lot of writing since their inception, academic writing on the international film festival circuit is in its infancy in comparison to other areas of film studies. During the 1990s the New Film Historicist writings of Thomas Elsaesser, Tom Gunning and Noël Burch shifted the focus of film studies away from the filmic text to the context in which films were produced, distributed, exhibited and received (de Valck 2007: 20). Individual essays by Bill Nichols (1994), Julian Stringer (2001; 2003) and Thomas Elsaesser (2005a) addressed aspects of the film festival experience and attempted to define the various agendas of both festivals and their attendees. Stringer identified the festival circuit as a global market in which each major festival follows a similar conceptual pattern whilst expressing its cultural difference (2001: 139), whilst Elsaesser suggested three sets of consistent indicators by which festivals could be assessed: 'festivals as event', 'distinction and value addition', and 'programming and agenda setting' (2005a: 94). The first of these indicators considers the short-term festival community in its location, the second the categorising of films and attendees within a hierarchy, and the third the negotiation between festival programmers and other bodies in determining the festival programme.

Concurrently, individual festivals began to publish their own histories, usually to commemorate a significant anniversary. Often written by festival insiders, such accounts are subjective anecdotal works. Indeed, one of the earliest examples is Forsyth Hardy's 1992 account of EIFF, *Slightly Mad and Full of Dangers*. Hardy was one of the founders of EIFF and active on the Executive Committee for 45 years. Certain other accounts of individual festivals, such as Kieron Corless and Chris Darke's study of Cannes (2007), have taken a more objective outsider's perspective backed up by access to festival archives and interviews with a wide range of participants.

Few books have been devoted entirely to a general assessment of the global festival circuit. Of those studied for this investigation, Kenneth Turan identifies three distinct festival agendas: Business, Geopolitics and Aesthetics (2002). The first category would include the major festivals such as Cannes, Venice, Berlin and Toronto; the second includes those events born out of a particular geopolitical situation, such as Sarajevo or Midnight Sun in Finland; and the third refers to events focusing on a particular film genre or area of cinema history, such as Pordenone. However, this somewhat ahistorical approach does not consider the possibility of festivals embracing two or three agendas at once, or of changing agenda over time. Cannes, Venice and Berlin can all be described as having geopolitical origins, whilst Sarajevo, first staged in 1995 during the Serbian siege of the city, has blossomed into a major event for the industry of South-East Europe. Nor does Turan's work explain festivals that arguably do not fit any of these three categories, EIFF included.

Marijke de Valck offers perhaps the most comprehensive evaluation of the film festival phenomenon to date. She first establishes three distinct historical stages of festival development: showcases of national cinemas (1932-circa 1970); independently organised 'protectors of the cinematic art' (the 1970s); and global professionalisation (1980s-the present) (2007: 19-20). I will expand on these categories in my own account. De Valck goes on to introduce concepts from sociology and anthropology, primarily Actor-Network Theory, to identify festivals as nodes within a network and to categorise the various entities present at each event – industry professionals, guests, audience, films, venues, trade magazines and newspapers – as actors on whose relationships to one another the network depends (2007: 30). Not unlike Turan, de Valck explores three levels on which festivals operate: Geopolitics, Business and Culture, with the latter subdivided into media/press and audiences/cinéphiles (2007: 16). However, considering the overlapping or competing agendas of the actors sustaining the network, de Valck understands that a single event cannot be defined purely in terms of one of these three levels, but rather incorporates all of them to varying degrees in order to function properly and maintain its position in the network.

Taking her lead from Elsaesser, de Valck explores concepts such as 'festival as event', 'agenda setting' and 'value addition' as indicators of a festival's output. De Valck theorises the interrelation between these concepts and explains how they function on both a spatial and a temporal level by taking into account both the competing agendas of the festival participants and those of the wider network of festivals. This allows for a greater understanding of the interdependence between 'actors' in the network, such as that between festivals and the media (2007: 125). Crucially, she identifies festivals as 'sites of passage' (2007: 36). This term delineates the festival as what Actor-Network theorists such as Bruno Latour view as an 'obligatory point of passage', an indispensable node in the network, while at the same time evoking the anthropological idea of 'rites of passage'. A rite of passage marks change in a social structure, 'a necessary suspension by means of ritualistic performance to mark a transition' (2007: 37), while the ritual generates value for its participants. De Valck argues that festivals perform a rite of passage through enacting widely recognised rituals and symbolic acts (red carpets, award ceremonies); the cultural value generated by the performance of the ritual elevates their status in the network. Through such gestures, the festival justifies its position as an obligatory point of passage:

> [Each] festival is an extended cultural performance during which 'other' rules of engagement count and the commercial market rules of the film world outside are suspended. It is my understanding that the survival of the phenomenon of film festivals and its development into a global and widespread festival circuit has been dependent on the creation of film festivals as a zone, a liminal state, where the cinematic products can bask in the attention they receive for their aesthetic achievements, cultural specificity, or social relevance. (De Valck 2007: 37)

In considering EIFF, the concept of a 'site of passage' becomes problematic. From its origins in 1947, EIFF has always foregone the familiar rituals and symbolic acts of the 'A-list' festivals. Edinburgh has, until comparatively recently, never been a competitive festival; even now it offers only a handful of awards in certain categories.[5] De Valck argues that festivals have sustained themselves through their willingness to facilitate 'secondary' interests, such as trade fairs, tourist attractions and city marketing (2007: 38). As we shall see, EIFF was established concurrently with, but independently from, the International Arts Festival of Edinburgh. This unique position of freedom from the financial and ideological constraints of such secondary interests allowed EIFF to generate different forms of cultural value, specifically critical discourses surrounding key issues of cinema (McArthur 1990: 100).[6] Whatever influence such discourses may have on wider film culture, it is difficult to consider them in terms of a currency of value addition on the festival circuit, nor can one easily define the extent to which EIFF authored such discourses. De Valck describes festivals as a product of the 'simultaneous activity of different sets of participants [...] each acting out their own unique performances rather than a collective script which could be identified and unravelled as a continuity' (2007: 32). In this light, it would be a mistake to merely equate a festival with the contribution/agenda of the Festival Director; instead it is necessary to consider the wider cultural context out of which EIFF's concerns grew.

Aside from annual press assessments, critical writing on the development of EIFF is limited at present. As an insider's account, Forsyth Hardy's 1992 work offers one revealing, if openly biased, perspective on EIFF programming in the 1970s and the achievements of that period. Three other works have been of value to this study. Lynne Stanford (2006) offers a broad overview, identifying five overlapping stages in the festival's then 60-year history: documentary to fiction (1947-63), filmmaker retrospectives (1964-81), representing the nation (1969-89), promoting productions (1991-96) and cinéphilia (1995-2006). Examining the tenure of Lynda Myles,

Stanford considers the role of the Artistic Director and the influence of her collaborators and the wider culture on programming decisions. However, she does not account for the shifts taking place on the international festival circuit after 1968, and whilst she charts the development of film theory and film culture during this period, she does not place it in a historical context. In particular, the period of filmmaker retrospectives (1964-81) is one of varying focus and therefore this category is of limited value.

Colin McArthur (1990) identifies EIFF's periods of ascendancy and decline. He argues that the Festival's early years from 1947 and the decade following 1968 were marked by commitment to a particular 'politics of cinema':

> At both the historical moments, the immediate post-war period and the decade or so from 1969, when Edinburgh's critical cutting edge was sharpest, there was the strongest possible sense of great issues being at stake (documentary/realist cinema versus more stylised, 'escapist' cinema; 'popular' versus 'high' art) with appropriately explicit critical discourses for advancing the arguments. (McArthur 1990: 100)

McArthur suggests that the Festival flagged in the 1950s and early 1960s and in the 1980s when tendering an ill-defined 'best' of world cinema (1990: 100). McArthur's assessment serves as an excellent basis for an investigation into EIFF's history; however it implies a coherence to the Festival's programming which fails to take full account of the wider culture or competing agendas of the various participants.

Paul Willemen (1980) charts the shifting focus of the Festival after 1968 and throughout the 1970s. Willemen was deeply involved with the Festival's project during this period and his short pamphlet, published by the Festival, is as much of interest as historical document as critical text.[7] However, his division of the Festival into three key periods provides the foundation for my own account. The first period constitutes 20 years of post-war liberal humanism, an improving mission imposed by the defenders of 'an aristocratic cult of personal taste' (Willemen 1980: 1). Willemen's second period begins in 1969 when 'a small group of cinéphiles' staged a Samuel Fuller retrospective and published an accompanying collection of essays. Willemen sees this act as the 'harnessing of cinéphilia to an oppositional culture', challenging the 'literary approach to cinema' (1980: 1). The following years saw a series of auteur retrospectives. The third period is marked by a shift in 1975 from auteurism to the understanding of film as ideological operation. My own account of the period describes more fully how each of these stages was reached, whilst endeavouring to consider events more objectively than Willemen's politically charged contemporary account.

In describing anthropologist Daniel Dayan's experience at the 1997 Sundance Film Festival, de Valck highlights the problem of methodology for film festival study (2007: 130-1). Quite apart from having to track the 'fragile equilibrium' of independent performances by the heterogeneous actors, Dayan discovered that a festival generates a wealth of printed material in a process of (self-)definition. In effect, the researcher must take into account a 'double festival: the visual and the written' (2007: 131). In the case of my historical study, the revised 'double festival' consists of the written and the oral. The written aspect consists of the texts outlined above, contemporary assessments in critical journals, and the Festival's own publications and private reports during this period. The oral includes my own interviews with key participants, but also unpublished transcripts of interviews conducted in 1986 and the Executive Committee meeting minutes of the period. Whilst I am aware of the limitations of such sources – interviews offer accounts that are one-sided, anecdotal or revised in hindsight, while minutes can only provide a condensed, mediated version of a discussion – they nevertheless give a sense of immediacy that written accounts cannot. By combining various sources, I have attempted to construct a sense of the diversity of agendas both within the Festival organisation itself and in the wider culture, whilst avoiding romanticising the contribution of any one individual. In the process I hope to give an account of a progressive institution, balancing founding principles with the need for persistent reinvention.

# Edinburgh and the European
# Film Festival Phenomenon

Following a period of localised, one-off events (e.g. Monaco, Turin, Hamburg, Prague), the first recurring film festival was founded in Venice in 1932. Initiated by Benito Mussolini, Venice was initially characterised by Fascistic theatrical splendour and a biased programming policy (Corless et al. 2007: 12). Cannes, established in 1939 by French diplomats and British and American film industry representatives but delayed by the Second World War, was intended as a corrective. The first edition in 1946 was a triumphant showcase, not least of American productions held back by the war (de Valck 2007: 49). Subsequently, several festivals emerged which shared certain characteristics. Funded by the state almost without exception, they were intended to promote international relations whilst showcasing the national industry. National delegations submitted their own selection of work to the programme, with the number of films to be screened relative to the size of that nation's output. In 1951 the Fédération International des Associations des Producteurs des Films (FIAPF) took on the role of regulating participating festivals. Concerned that the unmanaged spread of festivals would devalue the system of awards for its members, FIAPF formed a restricted 'A-list' of festivals permitted to hold an international jury competition. The organisation enforced this by instructing its members not to send their films to those festivals that did not participate (de Valck 2007: 54). Kieron Corless and Chris Darke write extensively of the problems inherent in this system and describe how, for example, the requirement that no film should cause offence to a represented nation led to compromises and diplomatic stand-offs (2007: 25-48).

Whilst at this period a singularly European phenomenon, established in no small part to balance domestic industries against the dominance of Hollywood product, the festival circuit nonetheless embraced Hollywood glamour. The presence of American stars was vital in attracting the international press that would in turn give exposure and prestige to the festival programme (de Valck 2007: 58). Ostensibly concerned with cultural enlightenment, festivals depended on the cooperation of international delegations, which looked to serve their own national interests. Thus festivals were both diplomatic mission and international trade fair. The case of the Berlin Film Festival, established in 1951, is of particular significance in this regard. Initiated by the post-war American administration in partnership with German industry figures, Berlin excluded Eastern European nations from participation, whilst favouring British and American product. In an aggressive policy of promoting Western values to the East, the Festival was scheduled to coincide with the International Youth Festival in Soviet-occupied East Berlin and films were screened in 21 cinemas along the border. When the Berlin Wall went up in 1961, the organisers broadcast the films in heavy rotation on local television instead (de Valck 2007: 52-3).

The case of Edinburgh was significantly different. With the support of John Grierson, founder of the British documentary movement, Edinburgh Film Guild members Norman Wilson and Forsyth Hardy staged the first Edinburgh Film Festival in 1947. Their action was effectively one of compensation for the exclusion of cinema from the newly founded and state-funded International Arts Festival (Hardy, Interview). The early focus was on documentary, albeit a broader definition of the term than is used now, primarily because it had been Scotland's main contribution to international film culture to date (F. Hardy 1950: 34). Forsyth Hardy has since spoken of a widespread 'tremendous hunger' in the post-war period to learn about the current state of other countries (Hardy, Interview). To feed that hunger, the Festival presented a diet of socially transformative films, visions of a future dedicated to public need. International delegates screened a selection of their national product to 'solemn young men' in a small Hill Street preview cinema and post-film discussions stimulated the assembled company to consider 'what their own contribution in the future might be' as co-founder Edgar Anstey put it (Antsey, Interview).

Whilst the Festival shared in spirit, therefore, the geopolitical concerns of the major post-war festivals, it was not governed by state interests, nor was it competitive. It was consequently not bound by the diplomatic constraints imposed on other festivals. The decision to specialise in documentary was a radical one, even if one can trace an element of pragmatism in the decision as without the state subsidies of its rivals or the cooperation of FIAPF, Edinburgh could not hope to compete in terms of glamour. Writing in 1950, Forsyth Hardy argued for greater specialisation of festivals, to 'bring some order into what everybody admits has become a confused and somewhat overcrowded field' (1950: 33). Specialisation gave Edinburgh a set of specific aims, to showcase international 'realist production' and 'to create an opportunity for the reconsideration and reassessment of the principles and methods' of documentary filmmaking (1950: 35). Conferences and screenings of Neorealist titles such as *Paisà* (Roberto Rossellini, Italy, 1946) and *La terra trema* (Luchino Visconti, Italy, 1948) served to develop or challenge the concept of documentary. From its earliest days, therefore, EIFF was making an explicit intervention into film culture quite unlike that of any other festival, both advocating and interrogating a specific politics of cinema whilst simultaneously reflecting a wide public interest.

# British Appreciation / French Desire

As the decade continued and film trends shifted away from realism, EIFF necessarily abandoned its documentary specialisation, officially embracing fiction, with Grierson's encouragement, in 1954 (F. Hardy 1992: 32). The serious consideration of film culture continued in a series of conferences on television, screenwriting and films for children (EIFF Brochures 1952-1957). However, as Lynne Stanford argues, this shift was not accompanied by a clear focus (2006: 16); throughout the 1950s the organisers continued to screen documentaries in broad groupings of subject matter, whilst donning black tie for occasional appearances by the likes of John Huston, Terry Thomas or Gene Kelly (Antsey, Interview).

Film culture in Britain between the Second World War and the mid-1960s followed a liberal humanist tradition of educating the widest possible public (Munro 2006: 110). In order to justify cinema as an art form in its own right, film criticism focused on a canon of European 'art cinema' directors whilst, with a few exceptions, the work of the American studios was considered commercial, low-cultural and therefore unworthy of study. The British Film Institute (BFI), in partnership with the explicitly apolitical British Federation of Film Societies (BFFS) (Selfe 2007: 84), created a network of Regional Film Theatres in order to distribute less commercial 'cultural' cinema and, tellingly, to liberate and recontextualise those art films that were performing perfectly well on the 'X and sex' circuit (Selfe 2007: 10).

The Festival of the early 1960s attempted to engage with liberal humanist arguments surrounding film as art. Under the directorship of Michael Elder, EIFF staged two themed programmes on Film and Literature (1962) and Film and Drama (1963). The first of these was based on the premise that 'a two-way traffic of ideas has developed which benefits both the printed word and the screen image' (EIFF Brochure 1962: 5), though the introductory text by *The Scotsman* critic Allen Wright offered no concrete example of how film had benefited literature other than in the sale of screen rights, whilst only the inclusion of *L'Année dernière à Marienbad* (*Last Year in Marienbad*, Alain Resnais, France/Italy, 1961) indicated any awareness of current formal advances in filmmaking. *The Herald*'s Molly Plowright, introducing the following year's programme, at least acknowledged the 'fundamental difference' between film and drama and touched on problems of language and adaptation in her anecdote about a Belgian colleague proclaiming Akira Kurosawa's Shakespeare adaptation  *Kumonosu-jô* (*Throne of Blood*, Japan, 1957) the 'finest Macbeth I have ever seen' (EIFF Brochure 1963: 5). However, in the absence of a specific engagement with the medium on its own terms, the unconscious implication of these years was that only those films associated with authors in the established arts are worthy of analysis.

The Festival made moves towards consideration of a bourgeois art cinema canon in the following years with modest retrospectives devoted to King Vidor (1964), Ingmar Bergman (1964), Fred Zinnemann (1965) and Andrzej Munk (1965). But the clearest indication of the absence of any clear focus is *Scottish Daily Express* critic Neville Garden's introductory text to the 1965 edition, which offers no engagement with any aspect of film culture other than celebrating the 'sense of purpose' and 'uniquely informal formality' of the Festival itself:

> It would be wrong, I think, to describe the festival's organisers as 'dedicated' [...] in spite of their zealous attempts to put cinema above all else. The word 'dedicated' suggests an almost fierce single-mindedness and lack of awareness of the world around them. 'Purposeful' fills the bill rather better. (Neville Garden, EIFF Brochure 1965: 5)

Meanwhile in France a 'fierce single-mindedness' had been driving cinéphiliac film culture for 15 years. Broadly characterised as the desire for cinema, the concept of cinéphilia emerged in France following the Second World War when a backlog of American films suddenly became available to Parisian audiences (Elsaesser 2005b: 30). Screened without discrimination in the chaotic yet religious aura of the Cinémathèque Française or the Cinéma MacMahon,[8] and viewed from a remove both spatial and temporal, the Hollywood studio films of the 1930s and 1940s took on, for some, a spiritual power. Such viewers' responses were 'framed by nostalgia and other retroactive temporalities, pleasures tinged with regret even as they [registered] as pleasure' (Elsaesser 2005b: 27). They collected fleeting moments of revelation, instants that triggered 'either the realisation or the illusion of a realisation that what is being seen is in excess of what is being shown' (Willemen 1994: 237). Willemen connects these moments of revelation to the radical disavowal of bourgeois norms expressed by French surrealism in the 1920s, 'the breathtaking fragment which suddenly and momentarily bore witness to the presence and force of desire in the midst of appallingly routinised and oppressive conditions of production' (1980: 2). As such they transcend the nakedly commercial basis on which these films were produced.

Cinéphilia can be understood as a response to the politically charged climate of post-war France, in which Hollywood was no more acceptable to the communist left than it was to the liberal-humanist bourgeois universities (MacCabe 1999: 151). The journal *Cahiers du cinéma* positioned itself in isolation from both academic and political engagement; it published personal responses to films, rather than judging them in relation to a humanist-literary canon or interrogating their ideologies (Willemen 1994: 235). Throughout the 1950s, under editor André Bazin *Cahiers* sought to 'liberate through education' (MacCabe 1999: 152) by evaluating the formal elements or cinematic means of popular film for a general audience. Bazin sought to release cinema from the confines of ideology, to demystify the filmmaking process and thereby suggest new possibilities for filmic expression. Cataloguing the fleeting moments of revelation they had collected in the cinema, the cinéphile *Cahiers* critics discovered key directors, or auteurs, working within the confines of the Hollywood studio system and celebrated the absence of intentionality on any level other than the mechanics of filmmaking in their films. Thus Sam Fuller could be fêted for 'having nothing at all to say' whilst European art directors were 'would-be philosophers who get into making films in spite of what film is, and who just repeat in cinema the discoveries of the other arts' (Luc Moullet, quoted in Caughie 1981: 43).

But the formulation of the 'politique des auteurs' created contradictions within the *Cahiers* project. The promotion of auteur-directors created a cult of personality around particular individuals, irrespective of the worth of specific films in their oeuvre or of the contribution of their collaborators. Furthermore, the competing claims of cinéphiles for this or that director's auteur status became an exclusionary discourse, intimating that only an initiated core audience could contribute to the debate. In 1957 Bazin offered a qualification of the politique des auteurs, warning that 'its exclusive practice leads to […] the negation of the film to the benefit of praise of its *auteur*':

> I feel that this useful and fruitful approach, quite apart from its polemical value, should be complemented by other approaches to the cinematic phenomenon which will restore to a film its quality as a work of art. This does not mean that one has to deny the role of the auteur, but simply give him back the presupposition without which the noun auteur remains but a halting concept. *Auteur*, yes, but what *of*? (Bazin, quoted in Caughie 1981: 46, italics in original)

This argument for a more inclusive approach to film analysis prefigured cinéphilia's political awakening during the 1960s. Several of the *Cahiers* critics were now practising filmmakers and whilst the Nouvelle Vague directors produced work on their own terms, they were obliged to confront the realities of the industry. As Colin MacCabe puts it, 'developments both national and international [produced] for these young, classical filmmakers a belated but none the less deeply felt modernism' (1999: 152). Modern Hollywood was destroying the studio system that had produced their heroes, whilst consumer society at home was eroding the Henri Langlois-inspired magic of the cinema-going experience (Ibid.). Jean-Luc Godard was the first to express the cinéphile's disillusionment in his critique of American influence on European filmmaking, *Le Mépris* (*Contempt*, France/Italy, 1963), but the significant cultural shift was to come five years later.

In Britain, the origins of a revolt against the liberal tradition of film appreciation can be traced to a contradiction uncovered by the work of the Society for Education in Film and Television (SEFT). Housed by the BFI, SEFT was an organisation devoted, through its journal *Screen Education* (reformed as *Screen* in 1969), to exploring practical issues of teaching film. Progressive educationalists wishing to promote the serious study of cinema found themselves obliged to adopt the stance of evaluating film by liberal humanist criteria as the 'product of a superior individual consciousness' (MacCabe 1985: 4). Yet their interest in popular cultural forms was directly opposed to this romantic art tradition. As the politique des auteurs filtered through from France, via the work of the American critic Andrew Sarris, the high-low cultural distinction between Europe and Hollywood began to be broken down. However, as we have seen, the auteurist approach remained focused on the 'superior individual consciousness', even if it was now that of the journeyman studio director, smuggling his artistry in through the back door. The flood of French theoretical ideas into British intellectual discourse in the aftermath of May '68 was to feed the negotiation of this contradiction.

# 1968: Cinéphilia / Theory / Festivals

When French students occupied overcrowded, anachronistic universities in May 1968, demanding new curricula and devolved powers, they effectively politicised questions about education and culture (MacCabe 1985: 5). Structural linguists Roland Barthes and Claude Lévi-Strauss had already begun the process of redefining the notion of 'culture', previously the domain of liberal humanist artistic expression, in terms of everyday experience (Munro 2006: 114). Given the language to politicise subjectivity, young Marxist intellectuals saw the opportunity to conflate class struggle with the struggle for ideas, transforming defeat on the streets into a struggle for control of cultural institutions. Simultaneously, politicised elements of the film industry took the struggle to the 'A-list' film festivals. In Edinburgh, the independence of the Festival from the restrictions of FIAPF and its origins in specialisation allowed a small group of cinéphile intellectuals to transform its agenda, realigning one of the oldest festivals with the new specialised events that acquired legitimacy following the events of that year.

The 'Langlois Affair', which started in February 1968, constituted a mobilisation in defence of cinéphilia. The Minister for Cultural Affairs André Malraux accused Henri Langlois of administrative inefficiency and archival incompetence and summarily removed him from his post as Director of the Cinémathèque Française. Within days attendees of the Cinémathèque mobilised to demonstrate against the government's action, supported by the Nouvelle Vague directors and several prominent philosophers, artists and international filmmakers. As Sylvia Harvey has stated, this was not a radical cause but a liberal one: the defence of a highly respected figure who, for many, was synonymous with the institution (1978: 15). Whether or not Malraux's accusations were justified, his intervention into the affairs of an independent organisation appeared heavy-handed and he was forced to back down.[9]

Significantly, this action served to set in place an organisational
infrastructure within the French film community, expediting the formation
of the Etats Généraux du Cinéma Français (EGC) three months later
(Harvey 1978: 15). An alliance of film technicians' unions, student
organisations, critics and filmmakers, which was formed in the wake of the
student-worker demonstration of 13 May 1968, the EGC called a total strike
of audiovisual workers, the first step towards a complete transformation
of the French film industry (Harvey 1978: 16). The EGC instructed Truffaut
and Godard to shut down Cannes, at that point halfway through its two-
week programme. Kieron Corless and Chris Darke give a full account of
the heated debates that followed (2007: 121-44), suggesting that Godard's
outburst towards a young cinéphile signified his final condemnation of
cinéphilia as an inadequate response to real political concerns:

> We're talking about solidarity with the students and workers
> and you're talking travelling shots and close-ups! You're a prick!
> (Godard, quoted in Corless et al. 2007: 131)

Paul Willemen has since declared that, in the sense of 'a particular
relationship to cinema […] [and] a particular historical period of relating to
cinema […] 1968 was more or less the end of cinéphilia' (1994: 227).

If 1968 saw the politicisation of cinéphilia and, according to Willemen,
the death of its initial form, over the following years the festival circuit
breathed new life into it. Although by 1969 *Cahiers* had transformed
itself into the 'official organ' of a newfound 'cinéphile disenchantment'
(Elsaesser 2005b: 34), the politique des auteurs retained currency for
a new generation of *Cahiers*-educated cinéphile festival programmers
promoting the work of individual filmmakers rather than reporting on
national outputs (de Valck 2007: 175). Young, non-competitive festivals
such as Pesaro and Rotterdam achieved prominence through a policy of
specialisation and serious cultural debate.[10] They were able to draw on

new cinema trends worldwide and on the entire film-historical canon in order to construct politically and culturally engaged programmes (de Valck 2007: 167). The Cannes disruption, followed by a similar protest at the Venice Film Festival in September, exposed the FIAPF-regulated system as antiquated, out-of-touch and artistically compromised. FIAPF's control of the 'A-list' festivals prevented the selection and promotion of independently produced work (Corless et al. 2007: 136). In a process of recuperation in response to (and thereby legitimising) the rise of the young thematic festivals, the 'A-list' events introduced quasi-independent sidebar events dedicated to new filmmakers, such as the Quinzaine des Réalisateurs at Cannes, a non-competitive showcase 'operating within rather than against the festival' (Corless et al. 2007: 135).

Concurrently, *Cahiers du cinéma*, in its transformed state, led the campaign to create politically and culturally engaged audiences through a programme of semiotics, psychoanalysis and Marxism, whilst Godard became the foremost practitioner of a theoretically-grounded activist film production that bypassed the dominant industry route (MacCabe 1999: 153). In Britain, young intellectuals found a solution to the contradictions of film as object of study by wedding the auteurism of *Cahiers du cinéma* and Andrew Sarris to newly adopted French structuralist theories. Thus a body of films could be analysed objectively and any consistencies understood 'in terms of underlying and unconscious structures […] rather than in the patently inappropriate terms of the romantic artist who intentionally and consistently expresses his own unique self' (Caughie 1981: 126).

Whether or not the tremors of the Cannes '68 crisis were felt in Edinburgh, the Festival was already undergoing its own transformation. The Festival at this time was funded by small grants from the City of Edinburgh Council and the Scottish Film Council (SFC) and was staffed on a largely voluntary basis. A system of selection by viewing committee held sway, relying almost entirely on submissions or on the recommendations of committee members viewing films whilst on holiday abroad (Grigor, Interview; EIFF

Executive Committee Minutes, 9 September 1967). The Festival's Executive and Viewing Committees consisted primarily of members of the Edinburgh Film Guild (EFG), the SFC and the Films of Scotland Committee (FSC).[11] The FSC naturally took an interest in the comparative output of other nations, and so indiscriminate national cinema days, formally presented by international delegations, continued to constitute a major part of the Festival programme. The Festival Director was employed by the FSC and effectively had to run the Festival in his spare time away from other responsibilities.

Murray Grigor, a young editor at the BBC, applied for the post of Festival Director in 1967 only to discover it was a lure for the post of Assistant Director of the FSC (Grigor, Interview). He had already been refused the opportunity to make his planned film on architect Charles Rennie Mackintosh, at that time a vilified figure, within the BBC and realised that taking the position at FSC might allow him to get his film made. In the event, he was only released from his FSC duties three weeks before the 1967 Festival to act as 'Director' of a largely pre-selected programme. He attempted to energise the programme by screening UK premières of a brazenly commercial work, *The Dirty Dozen* (Robert Aldrich, U.S./UK, 1967), and a politically sensitive one, *La battaglia di Algeri* (*The Battle of Algiers*, Gillo Pontecorvo, Italy/Algeria, 1966).[12]

Clearly, under these circumstances the Festival Director could exercise no significant control over the programme. Grigor's subsequent action indicates his intention to transform the organisation. On 4 September 1967, *The Scotsman* published a letter from a student, David Will, proclaiming the Festival 'second to none in its dullness' (1967: 6). A key figure at the Edinburgh University Film Society, Will complained of the Festival's selection by 'geographical distribution rather than cinematic quality,' and of the preponderance of short information films made by commercial or state interests. Grigor embraced Will and his girlfriend Lynda Myles on the strength of their ideas, co-opting them into the Festival staff in the spring of 1968 (Myles, Interview).

Whilst Grigor was a practising filmmaker, Will and Myles were self-declared cinéphiles in the French tradition. After developing an early interest in European Art cinema, Will remembers his first viewing of *Red River* (Howard Hawks, U.S., 1948), whilst still at school, as an 'epiphany' (Will, Interview). Rejecting the liberal arts orthodoxy of the BFI-funded magazine *Sight and Sound*, he read the French journals *Cahiers du cinéma* and *Positif*, and the British auteurist journal *Movie*. He met Myles in his first week at university. Soon they had taken over the film society, screening nine films each week in order to educate themselves. Bypassing London altogether, they began visiting Paris, where they would attend five films a day at the Cinémathèque Française under the personal guidance of Henri Langlois (2008c).[13]

Will remembers their most radical step in 1968 being the decision to actually invite films to the Festival (Will, Interview). However, their choice of titles is also significant. Prolific Hollywood B-movie director Roger Corman was represented for the first time with screenings of *The Wild Angels* (U.S., 1966) and *The Trip* (U.S., 1967), as well as the film he financed for young critic-turned-director Peter Bogdanovich, *Targets* (U.S., 1968). As Forsyth Hardy later remarked, 'Corman was to become as much an "Edinburgh" director as [Ingmar] Bergman' (1992: 96). The comparison with Bergman is a telling one. Myles claims she and Will knew the writings of Andrew Sarris word-for-word (Myles, Interview). Sarris' refinement of the politique des auteurs constituted the first English language defence of the studio directors. In 1962 he argued that the relative freedom of European art directors to pursue their own projects led to a disjuncture between insight and cinematic expression. Using Bergman as an example, he wrote:

> A [George] Cukor, who works with all sorts of projects, has a more
> developed abstract style than a Bergman, who is free to develop
> his own scripts. Not that Bergman lacks personality, but his work
> has declined with the depletion of his ideas largely because his
> technique never equalled his sensibility. (Sarris 1979: 662-3)

The decision to screen three Corman titles, therefore, was a clear indication that Grigor, Myles and Will wished to steer the festival away from European art cinema towards an auteurist engagement with popular forms.

Grigor recognised that without the funds to compete with other festivals on their terms, Edinburgh had not only to satisfy audiences but also to give the critics something worth writing about – what he terms 'writeability' – in order to maintain a significant position internationally (Grigor, Interview). Will saw it in more stark terms: 'It may sound arrogant, but we [Grigor, Myles and Will] weren't really interested in the general audience. We were interested in the critics writing about what we were doing; we were making a cultural intervention' (Will, Interview). Positive press coverage would also strengthen Grigor's position against the protests of the Executive and Viewing Committees, who were soon to express concerns about being sidelined (EIFF Executive Committee Minutes, 17 September 1969). For the 1969 Festival, Grigor supported Will's idea to stage a complete retrospective honouring Sam Fuller, the sensationalist studio director heavily fêted by the pre-'68 *Cahiers du cinéma*, but almost unknown in the UK.[14] Accused by members of the Executive Committee of bringing the festival into disrepute, Grigor defended his decision by justifying Fuller's work in terms that the Griersonian old guard would appreciate – on the basis of its subject matter. He argued, for example, that *Steel Helmet* (U.S., 1951) was the first film to explore racial tension in the U.S. military and that *Pickup on South Street* (U.S., 1953) unpacked the concept of McCarthyism (Grigor, Interview).

At the suggestion of *Movie* critic Charles Barr, Will approached Peter
Wollen for help in staging the retrospective. Wollen's *Signs and Meaning
in the Cinema*, published that year, was the first expression of the project
to combine auteur theory with French structuralism. Wollen was a recent
recruit to the BFI's Education Department and became instrumental in
devising a policy of promoting film studies as an academic discipline to
the universities (MacCabe 1999: 155). Wollen co-edited a book of essays
on Fuller, to which 15 critics and filmmakers contributed (Will et al. 1969).
The impact of the Fuller retrospective was unprecedented in the Festival's
history, prompting a subsequent Fuller season at the National Film Theatre
in London, two further critical studies devoted to the director (P. Hardy
1970; Garnham 1971), and, thanks in no small part to the garrulous Fuller's
presence,[15] the best publicity EIFF had received since its earliest years (EIFF
Executive Committee Minutes, 17 September 1969).

1969 also saw a focus on Corman's films for American International
Pictures,[16] the UK première of *Easy Rider* (Dennis Hopper, U.S., 1969) and
sidebars devoted to the avant-garde, graphics and pop films. Will screened
*Pierrot le fou* (Jean-Luc Godard, France/Italy, 1965) to illustrate Godard's
debt to Fuller. However, when Will invited Godard to participate in the
Fuller event, he refused in no uncertain terms (Grigor, Interview) – an act
which can be seen as exemplifying the cinéphile disenchantment of the
new *Cahiers du cinéma*. Whilst the 1969 EIFF programme constituted one of
the earliest negotiations of auteurism by a British film institution, Grigor,
Myles and Will had yet to generate the sort of critical discourse that could
be seen as an active participation in political struggle. With no diplomatic
interests at stake for the Festival organisation, the Edinburgh cinéphiles'
coup d'état had been achieved without the disruptions seen elsewhere.
However, the 1970 edition saw a crisis that almost bankrupted the Festival.
Exposed to the realities of the film industry, Myles and Will's cinéphilia
was to become increasingly politicised in the years that followed.

# The Politicisation of Edinburgh's Cinéphilia

As we have seen, the transformation of EIFF in 1969 merely reflected French cinéphile interests that had already been repudiated by the transformed *Cahiers du cinéma*. The following year saw the Festival's first experience of censorship (F. Hardy 1992: 103) and the resulting financial crisis almost put an end to the cinéphile project. But the reinvention of *Screen* as a theoretical journal in 1971 was to give the programming team a new language with which to politicise their film interests and consolidate the Festival's international standing. In 1973 the position of Festival Director was made a fulltime post, effectively formalising the changes the organisation had undergone since 1968.

The EIFF Executive Committee applauded the programming team for the outstanding publicity generated by the 1969 event but voiced concern that Grigor had not heeded opinions expressed in the committee viewing sessions (EIFF Executive Committee Minutes, 17 September 1969). There is a sense from the programme of the following year that Grigor gave Will and Myles freedom to pursue as many of their interests as possible. In addition to an extensive retrospective devoted to Nouvelle Vague director Claude Chabrol, there was a tribute to Darryl F. Zanuck and Twentieth Century Fox,[17] two new Corman titles,[18] a retrospective introducing another young American B-movie director, Monte Hellman, and the first attempt at opening a discourse on British auteur practice with the screening of three of Terence Fisher's Dracula films for Hammer Productions.[19] Will also collaborated with another young theorist, Paul Willemen, on the publication of a collection of essays devoted to Roger Corman (Will et al. 1970).

However, the 1970 edition was to provoke considerable controversy, both within and outside the Festival organisation. The young cinéphile programmers were forced to confront commercial realities much as French cinéphile filmmakers had done over the preceding decade (MacCabe 1999: 152). Forsyth Hardy describes a censorship battle between EIFF and Edinburgh city magistrates over several uncertificated titles (1992: 103), notably the Shelly Winters crime spree picture *Bloody Mama* (Roger Corman, U.S., 1970). In part this controversy blew up, ironically, because of Grigor's conscientiousness. As no formal agreement had ever been reached regarding the screening of uncertificated films, Grigor submitted the six potentially contentious titles to the magistrates for consideration. Several magistrates condemned *Bloody Mama* before viewing it and the local press got hold of the story. With the Festival team putting all their energy into battling for permission to go ahead with the screenings, marketing was neglected and ticket sales suffered dramatically (EIFF Executive Committee Minutes, 12 September 1970). However, of greater significance are the events surrounding *O.K.* (Michael Verhoeven, West Germany, 1970).

Taking a Brechtian approach to contemporary politics, *O.K.* displaces the true story of the rape of a Vietnamese girl by U.S. soldiers to a Bavarian setting. The film had brought the 1970 Berlin Film Festival to a premature end when the American jury members used outdated FIAPF regulations to justify sidelining it from award consideration. De Valck describes how the resulting controversy forced the Berlin Film Festival organisers to reform, just as Cannes and Venice had done two years previously (2007: 64-6). Nothing less than artistic independence was at stake and Berlin finally shook off the constraints of its geopolitical origins as a showcase of Western values. As an independent festival, Edinburgh's programme was not constrained by diplomatic considerations; Grigor considered himself beholden only to the city magistrates. However, unforeseen pressure came from the American distributor of *Bloody Mama*, who threatened to pull Corman's film if 'such an anti-American work' was shown (Will, Interview). Grigor decided he couldn't afford to alienate the American studios and cancelled the screening of *O.K.* This incident was arguably the cinéphile programmers' first direct experience of Hollywood's considerable clout in the market and thus it paved the way for the increasing politicisation of the Festival throughout the 1970s.

The loss of income from ticket sales almost shelved the 1971 Festival and gave the committee cause to express a range of fears about the way the programme was heading. In an ironic near-reversal of the Berlin situation, criticisms were voiced of the lack of geographical spread and the absence of national cinema days (EIFF Executive Committee Minutes, 12 September 1970). When Murray Grigor suggested that the Festival apply to the BFI for funding, the committee refused in no uncertain terms (EIFF Executive Committee Minutes, 25 January 1971). This refusal should be considered in the context of the 1970 rupture at the BFI over the Education Department's proposed policy of intervening in academic institutional discourses to establish film as an object of serious study.[20] The liberal humanist Festival founders would naturally be suspicious of a politicised film study culture.

The 1971 edition was a comparatively low-key event, designed with the intention of avoiding any further debts or controversy.[21] Neither Will nor Myles took part (Myles, Interview). In November, Forsyth Hardy and two other key committee members, having steered the Festival back into the black, intimated their intention of resigning. Hardy 'no longer felt in accord with the kinds of enthusiasms being expressed in sections of the cinema' (EIFF Executive Committee Minutes, 23 November 1971). However they were persuaded to phase out their departures to avoid the appearance of a mark of no confidence. The Chairman and the Honorary Treasurer left office shortly after, while Forsyth Hardy chose instead to retain his seat on the committee well into the 1980s, fighting a rearguard action against these 'enthusiasms'. The departures provided Grigor with an opportunity to introduce Colin Young to the committee. A pioneer of observational documentary, Young had recently been appointed to set up the National Film and Television School (NFTS) at Beaconsfield. An 'arch-liberal', according to Myles (Myles, Interview), on taking the committee Chairmanship, Young nevertheless became a powerful ally first of Grigor, then Myles, seeing his role as 'running protection' for them against the more conservative elements of the committee (Young, Interview).

During the same year, the newly independent SEFT re-launched *Screen* as a theoretical journal promoting the systematic study of film over subjective appreciation in a 'collective effort to link formal analyses of film to political perspectives' (MacCabe 1985: 9). Substantial portions of the early editions were devoted to translations of new French theory and of older European material as yet unavailable in Britain (Munro 2006: 116). Brecht's writings and psychoanalytic theory were applied to film in order to explore problems around the relationship between the social and the individual. Lacan's work on the impossibility of stabilising subject and meaning was seen as particularly useful since the filmic text could be understood not as 'the representation of the author's psychic conflict but […] the enactment of a series of conflicts shared by author and reader' (MacCabe 1985: 8). In an Althusserian Marxist political context, this concept of unfixed subjectivity was seen as a revolt against the dominant bourgeois ideology of closure and fixed identity.

Whilst much important work was achieved via this approach to film analysis, particularly in the feminist writing of Laura Mulvey and Claire Johnston, considerable criticism has since been levelled at this period. Suggestions have been made that many intellectuals were merely using cinema as a tool to dislodge the dominant liberal humanist ideology in academic institutions,[22] or that they applied an incomplete form of structuralist and psychoanalytic theory (Caughie 1981: 124; Willemen 1994: 225). Nevertheless, in the following years, the concerns of *Screen* were echoed in the shifting focus of the EIFF programmers, who collaborated closely with several of the journal's contributors (Myles, Interview).

This collaboration was already apparent in 1972, which saw the return of Will and Myles' cinéphilia in a mature, politicised form. That year's Douglas Sirk retrospective reflected *Screen*'s own declared interest in the

neglected director.[23] Alongside this retrospective, Myles staged the first
European festival event devoted to female directors, working closely with
theoreticians Laura Mulvey and Claire Johnston (Myles, Interview).[24]
Mulvey has acknowledged this conference as a landmark in feminist
film studies, describing the experience of critics and filmmakers working
together as 'opening the floodgates of questions, questioning everything:
questioning relations of power around the cinema, women as spectacle,
the dominance of Hollywood' (Mulvey, Interview). The combination of
the Sirk retrospective and the Women's Event marked the first significant
interrogation of cinéphilia's gender politics and its unquestioning
promotion of (white) heterosexual male directors. The retrospective drew
attention to Sirk's strategy of smuggling a pessimistic vision of frustrated
dreams and concealed desires into lavish melodramas (EIFF Brochure 1972:
4) while the Women's Event sought not merely to pay homage to female
directors in a man's cinema,[25] but to ask 'what would a women's cinema be
like?' (EIFF Brochure 1972: 7). When a BBC crew came to cover the event,
the delegates insisted on shooting the film themselves, taking the means of
production into their own hands and challenging what Mulvey was to term
the 'male gaze' (Mulvey, Interview).

The following year Grigor passed the directorship to Myles.[26] When the
Scottish Film Council agreed to employ her and then second her to EIFF
she became, effectively, the first full-time Director of the Festival, (EIFF
Executive Committee Minutes, 7 July 1973). Her appointment came at a
time in which, in reaction to FIAPF's heavy-handed attempts to retain
control of the festival circuit, independent festivals became increasingly
organised. FIAPF was threatening to withhold 'films of quality' from
Edinburgh unless the Festival paid a registration fee of $1000, a figure
EIFF simply couldn't afford (Executive Committee Minutes, 7 July 1973).
Myles became involved in the creation of the Fédération Internationale
des Festivals Independents (FIFI), which consisted of the new sidebar
festivals created at Cannes and Berlin (the Quinzaine des Réalisateurs
and the Young Forum respectively) alongside Edinburgh, Rotterdam and

other festivals (Myles, Interview). This alliance allowed the independent events to share information about international cinemas not controlled by FIAPF.[27] It is clear from these events, therefore, that Cannes did not 'set the template' (Elsaesser 2005a: 90) for Edinburgh's reinvention; rather that the creation of a fulltime director came about in the wake of a successful new programming policy inspired by theoretical advances and supported by contact with other independent international festivals.

# The Limits of Auteurism

The 1974 retrospective marked a turning point in the Festival's negotiation
of auteur theory and heralded Willemen's third period of development
for the Festival, in which auteur retrospectives were replaced by a series
of theoretical events founded on the consideration of film as ideological
operation (Willemen 1980: 1). Through this process, Myles and her
collaborators briefly established an annual programme designed around
a coherent stance in opposition to mainstream film culture in Britain.
However, with greater critical regard came the need to professionalise
and increase expenditure. The poorly funded Festival organisation could
not meet such demands. Faced with opposition within the Executive
Committee to what were seen as elitist events and without the support of
*Screen*, whose influence by 1977 had been reduced by vicious in-fighting,
Myles was forced to revert to a more populist, less critically defined
approach to programming in the latter years of the decade.

Selecting the work of the 'widely ranging and inconsistent' (F. Hardy
1992: 123) Raoul Walsh for the 1974 retrospective and screening over
50 titles (a mere third of his total output), Myles and her collaborator
Phil Hardy wilfully threw into question the notion of a common thread
running through a studio director's work. Forsyth Hardy's response was
typically scathing. Having seen Walsh's work 'in the normal course of
events as a film critic', he could remember none 'that were notable in any
way at all' (Hardy, Interview). Mainstream critics shared his reaction and
Barry Norman famously took the trouble to discredit the accompanying
publication on primetime television (MacCabe 1975: 128).

Mainstream liberal film culture expected a retrospective to argue the case
for a neglected director's inclusion in the international film art canon.
However, Myles and Hardy's concern was less with Walsh himself than
with the very concept of auteurism. The choice of Walsh represented an

unequivocal statement of the position towards which EIFF retrospectives had been heading since 1969: that Hollywood film could be studied not for its intrinsic quality (however this might be defined), but rather to identify the various structures that combined to create its meaning. Walsh's work was used to examine issues of film criticism, narrative structure, the studio system and the representation of women in cinema (P. Hardy 1974: 7).

Since the Women's Event of 1972 the Festival programme had reflected an increasing interest in questions of screen representation and the implicit power relations contained by cinéphilia. Laura Mulvey's essay 'Visual Pleasure and Narrative Cinema', published in *Screen* in 1975, encapsulated these concerns. As Willemen remarks, such questions 'forced film theory into a fundamental reassessment of the relations between text and audience' (1980: 2). This fresh approach was consolidated the following year in the Jacques Tourneur retrospective, which explicitly '[did] not propose a new author to be discovered, but a series of texts' through which wider questions of film culture could be considered (EIFF Brochure 1975: 5). Colin MacCabe's contemporary comments in *Screen* on the mainstream reaction to the Walsh retrospective are indicative of the politically charged climate surrounding film culture in Britain at the time. MacCabe suggested that the book of essays vilified by Barry Norman represented a threat because it broke down the 'division of labour' between academics and popular intellectuals – which presumably included Norman – rendering redundant the latter's role as adaptor/translator for the masses (1975: 133). This is not to say that advanced theoretical work of the time would reach a wide audience, as MacCabe acknowledged (1975: 129), but rather that examining a popular cultural form in this manner was to bring theory and practice into a closer relationship. To suggest that 'film studies cannot be extricated from [...] the real political struggles of the present' was to constitute 'a decisive threat to the liberal petty-bourgeois interest in film' (MacCabe 1975: 133). Reflecting the discourse of *Screen* at the time, MacCabe concluded that theoretical work on film should capitalise on this advance by actively engaging with 'the actual areas of struggle in the cinema – particularly the increasing use of film as agit material' (1975: 134). Over the following three years, Myles broke from the pattern of (auteur) retrospectives to stage theoretical conferences in partnership with *Screen*.[28]

The first of these considered the implications of Bertold Brecht's work for a political cinema. This followed an entire edition of *Screen* devoted to Brecht the previous year (1974). Brecht had proved newly relevant to post-'68 theorists grappling with 'the tripartite relationship between textual properties, contemporary social reality and historically formed readers' (Harvey 1982: 51). The conference focused on three distinct areas: Brecht's own work in the cinema, recent experimental forms of political cinema, and the influence of Brecht on British film and television. Two films were screened each afternoon and a related paper presented the following morning.[29] Of common concern to all three strands was a consideration of film as ideological operation, a critique of 'the reactionary effects of the dominant cinema' (EIFF Brochure 1975: 4). Forsyth Hardy describes the attendees as 'about sixty diehards' (1992: 126) and members of the seminar audience expressed an awareness that they might be considered 'a small clique discussing abstract theoretical questions' (Brewster 1975: 11). Nevertheless the selection of films accompanying the conference proved to be the biggest box-office draw of any retrospective by the Festival and an unprecedented 251 delegates and members of the press flocked to Edinburgh (EIFF Executive Committee Minutes, 31 October 1975). The consequent high spend on hospitality led to considerable outstanding debts and Chairman Colin Young announced that he had held discussions with representatives of the BFI regarding funding the Festival, reasoning that the London Film Festival, directly funded by the BFI, had been taking its lead from Edinburgh's programme for several years (EIFF Executive Committee Minutes, 19 May 1976).

That both the committee and the BFI were prepared to consider such a proposal only five years after Murray Grigor's similar suggestion had been rebuffed can be seen in part as an indication of the growing mainstream acceptance of the value of film study culture. Myles concedes that without the support of the liberal press, she would not have been allowed to continue. She courted mainstream critics such as Derek Malcolm (*The Guardian*) and David Robinson (*The Times*), even though she was criticised by the *Screen* critics for 'sleeping with the enemy' (Myles, Interview). Malcolm, in turn, remembers 'we were all furiously [...] thinking she was doing a terrible job or thinking she was doing a wonderful job. It's the sort of festival where you went to have a damn good argument about the programme' (Malcolm, Interview). However, events following the 1976 conference were to demonstrate just how far mainstream patience could be stretched and consequently how much influence the dominant cultural discourse would have on the Festival's direction.

The 1976 *Screen*-sponsored conference took its lead from questions raised at the Brecht conference about relations between film and viewer and the film text's construction of the reader. The application of psychoanalytic theory as the 'science of the construction of the individual' (EIFF Brochure 1976: 5) was the focus of the event, which featured nine films ranging from classic Hollywood drama to contemporary avant-garde works.[30] A second event focusing entirely on avant-garde film and inspired by the publication of Peter Wollen's essay 'The Two Avant-Gardes' (1975) brought together critics and practitioners of each of the two strands identified by Wollen. This forum sought to 'explore the points of similarity and difference' between what Wollen defined as the American non-narrative Co-op movement and the European political avant-garde within narrative cinema (EIFF Brochure 1976: 6). The two events were joined in a single publication edited by Phil Hardy, Claire Johnston and Paul Willemen, the *Edinburgh '76* magazine, which included the papers delivered at the psychoanalysis event alongside Wollen's article.

The magazine's introduction, written by Phil Hardy, Claire Johnston and Paul Willemen, situated EIFF outside traditional concepts of a film festival as liberal arts showcase or marketplace, declaring that 'the key issue at stake was film as an ideological practice':

> This change of emphasis, from the traditional notion of film as a form of cultural consumption, to one of meaning-production (stressing the practice of reading films) exposes a problem suppressed by the majority of film festivals. It is essential, if the festival is to continue to make a progressive critical intervention in British film culture, to move from a notion of consumption to one of production, with the act of filming and the act of reading being seen as two moments of equal value, neither having priority over the other. (Hardy et. al 1976: 3-4)

This shift from consumption to production was echoed in the aims of the avant-garde forum. Peter Wollen has since acknowledged that his article and the subsequent EIFF forum were intended to 'combine New York modernism with Parisian (68) theory', to bring together militant and formalist filmmakers in order to lay the theoretical foundations for the recently established Independent Filmmakers Association (1981: 9). These radical attempts to redefine the role of a film festival based on 'the dialectic of making/viewing' (Hardy et. al 1976: 5) were ultimately constrained, as we shall see, by the demands made of EIFF by the wider film culture, the international festival circuit, and members of its own Executive Committee. As Donald Macpherson remarked in his *Screen* discussion of the 1976 Festival, EIFF 'is held within the very contradictions which it foregrounds, its critical discourse part of that renewal and stabilisation of the cinematic institution' (1976/77: 110).

Reporting to the Executive Committee on the 1976 Festival, Myles was able to announce a 20 per cent rise in box office and a 33 per cent rise in press and delegates attending. Great enthusiasm had been expressed by some of the 100-plus participants of the psychoanalysis event (with similar events

already scheduled to take place in Italy and the U.S.), and by many of the
130 attendees of the avant-garde event. The funders of the latter event, the
Arts Council Film Committee, had expressed their satisfaction and there
had been 'a high degree of interest' from staff of various departments
of the BFI, including the National Film Theatre and the London Film
Festival. Finally, press coverage had been, she stated, 'on balance,
extremely favourable from the more serious journals and newspapers'
(EIFF Director's Report, November 1976). Myles sought to consolidate the
Festival's position by proposing a raft of measures to professionalise EIFF,
requesting a larger staff and a greater hospitality budget (EIFF Executive
Committee Minutes, 26 November 1976). Her suggestions reflected
the increasingly competitive nature of the festival circuit and the need,
therefore, to attract filmmaker guests with hospitality that could equal their
experience of other festivals (Myles, Interview).

Forsyth Hardy, however, objected to her proposals, submitting a vitriolic
critique to the committee, several of whom shared his views (F. Hardy
1976), and in his 1992 account of the festival he makes no secret of
his disapproval of the Festival's theoretical work during this period.
Considering the severity of his attack on the programming policy in
the meeting of 26 November that year and the Festival's subsequent
retreat from the position outlined in the *Edinburgh '76* introduction, some
consideration of this is necessary, particularly since Hardy's 1992 account
arguably misrepresents the circumstances. It is clear that Hardy felt the
Festival was in danger of losing sight of what he saw as its main objective:
'to make available to as large an audience as possible films distinguished
by imagination or experiment which otherwise they might not have been
able to see and by so doing to encourage their production' (1992: 130).
He quotes several negative reports in the mainstream media that dwell
on the apparent elitist, jargon-heavy nature of the conferences, in order
to support this concern. However, in stating that 'the blunt reality was
that if audiences were insufficient at the box-office to give the festival a
sound economic basis […] it could not continue' (1992: 130), he implies

that the theoretical work put box-office returns in jeopardy. He ignores the unquestionable material success of the 1976 Festival, of which the two theoretical events comprised a small but significant part.

Whether or not Hardy was reacting against the *Edinburgh '76* manifesto at the November committee meeting, he expressly questioned the judgement of the Festival directorate (F. Hardy 1976) . Whilst he could not criticise the programme on grounds of reduced box-office, he attacked Myles' proposals for increased expenditure and called into question the propriety of the Executive Committee's operations. He argued that the Festival was in no position financially to overhaul staffing or expenditure, reminded Myles that she had yet to be formally approved as director for the following year, and even went so far as to accuse the committee of failing to fulfil the terms of the Festival's constitution, calling for the reinstatement of practises that had widely been accepted to be obsolete, such as holding regular meetings of a selection committee (Ibid.).

The attack should be seen in the context of spiralling costs at a time when the Festival and other film bodies were raising funds for the purchase and renovation of a new site for the city's independent cinema, Filmhouse, in a derelict church on Lothian Road (EIFF Executive Committee Minutes, 1976-79). It is indicative also of a lack of understanding of the burgeoning film festival circuit. Hardy could not understand why the mere honour of a screening at Edinburgh was no longer enough to attract a filmmaker, or why the Festival could not rely on a largely voluntary workforce (F. Hardy 1976). He was also suspicious of the worth of Myles' trips to other international festivals and requested that she deliver reports to the committee on her return (EIFF Executive Committee Minutes, 26 November 1976). She agreed to do so and her report on Toronto later that year emphasised the new Canadian festival's self-confessed debt to Edinburgh's recent programming. The Toronto programmers identified Edinburgh as one of the world's six leading festivals, alongside Cannes, Karlovy-Vary, Berlin, Taormina and Los Angeles: 'The influence of

Edinburgh on the programme selection and structure was strongly marked in comparison to the other festivals. It appeared that the EIFF had been selected for three reasons: 1) its focus on special events and its strong record on retrospectives; 2) its policy of publications; 3) its commitment to young American directors' (Myles 1977a).[31]

Hardy also requested that Myles draw up a policy statement (EIFF Executive Committee Minutes, 7 March 1977). The resulting document contains shades of the *Edinburgh '76* manifesto in a diluted form yet it crucially enabled two generations of Festival staff to find a common ground. The document states that the Festival is 'committed to a serious approach to film culture,' a guiding principle that 'immediately and consistently distinguishes the EIFF from the vast majority of other film festivals which appear to be governed exclusively or predominately by considerations of commerce and tourism' (Myles 1977b). Hardy contributed ideas towards that year's conference, entitled History/ Production/Memory, and there were signs of compromise in the accompanying publication edited by Claire Johnston, *Edinburgh '77*, which appeared to address a wider readership (F. Hardy 1992: 132).

However, this compromise came at a cost. The History/Production/ Memory conference attempted to consider 'the question of ideology as a social instance involving questions of industry and institutions at a particular conjuncture' (EIFF Brochure 1977: 5-6). In doing so, it aimed to rethink what is meant by 'making a theoretical intervention in film culture' (Ibid.). This introspective approach appears quite at odds with the tone of the previous year's event introduction and various commentators remarked on the event's failure to 'grasp the object for discussion' (Whitaker 1978: 41; Nash et al. 1977/78: 77). The event included three separate film strands: state-sponsored production in Britain in the 1930s, Soviet film of the 1920s and British studio production of the 1940s and 1950s.[32] Discussion in Executive Committee meeting minutes gives the impression that this event evolved from diverse suggestions, not least

Hardy's own interest in Soviet cinema (EIFF Executive Committee Minutes, 3 May 1977). A planned Dziga Vertov retrospective was partially subsumed within the History / Production / Memory programme. Unusually, whilst several of Vertov's works were screened outside the theoretical event, the Festival brochure gave no introduction to his work, as had been the case with all previous retrospectives.[33] Where the previous two conferences had been created with specific aims and in close partnership with *Screen* critics, this event seemed to lack clear authorship or intent.

This conference came at a time of crisis for *Screen*. Four of the journal's board members resigned over what they saw as film theory's increasing exclusivity (MacCabe 1985: 11). Myles remembers vicious feuds surrounding the journal's use of Lacanian psychoanalytic theory, which was blamed for undoing all that had been achieved for secondary education and popular culture (Myles, Interview). By attaching value only to those works that broke with a so-called bourgeois ideology of closure, it was argued, theorists had rejected the same popular / commercial works that they had once embraced in favour of increasingly complex and demanding texts. Hollywood cinema was now considered to 'deprive the spectator of any perspective for social or political action except for privileged moments when vision was fleetingly disturbed by a pressure the text could not contain.' (MacCabe 1985: 11). This was seen by the four resigning board members as a retreat back into the 'high art enclave' from which film theorists had originally sought to escape.[34]

One of the positive results of the crisis was the re-launch of *Screen Education*, the SEFT-published journal that had preceded *Screen*. Whilst *Screen* foundered, *Screen Education* reinvigorated the progressive work in the areas of secondary education and popular forms such as Hollywood (MacCabe 1985: 12). The split between *Screen* and *Screen Education* is mirrored at the EIFF events in 1977. Whilst the History / Production / Memory event foundered on an inability to precisely define the terms of its own discussion, the concurrent Television event flourished.[35] Works by Peter Watkins and John McGrath were screened alongside *Brimstone & Treacle* (Barry Davis, UK, 1976), Dennis Potter's banned play about the Devil seducing a physically challenged girl (EIFF Brochure 1977: 100). The debates surrounding censorship in television had a heatedness and urgency that the History/Production/Memory event lacked, even if the combination of theorists and television practitioners inevitably resulted in a certain degree of mutual misunderstanding (Caughie 1977/78: 105).

Considering de Valck's notion of 'sites of passage' (2007: 36), it is possible to understand the period of theoretical debates as necessarily short-lived. Whilst I have argued that de Valck's theory is of limited application to an event whose cultural value cannot be defined in terms of a currency of awards and recognisable rituals, it is clear that by expressly refusing to trade in this currency, the Festival alienated itself from key actors within the network on whom each event relies, namely the mainstream liberal media and its own Executive Committee. At the same time, the Festival's reliance on a third group of actors, the theoretical critics, led to jeopardy when that group collapsed. The new focus on television was to anticipate a period in which the Festival necessarily addressed concerns of mainstream film culture, namely the rise in British production.

# Years of Uncertainty

Lynda Myles suggests that the theoretical work of the mid-1970s grew in part out of the British production vacuum of the period (Myles, Interview). The last years of the decade saw a modest resurgence in production, due in part to the formation of the Association of Independent Producers (AIP), which was committed to maintaining 'an indigenous industry' (EIFF Brochure 1978: 6), and EIFF reflected this in its programming. The 1978 edition included a one-day conference organised by the AIP alongside a focus on new British avant-garde production. The 1979 edition received press attention for the high concentration of new British feature-length and medium-length productions (Myles, Interview).[36] A Feminism and Cinema event was also staged the same year. Whilst the 1972 Women's Cinema event had emphasised theoretical research based on existing productions by female directors, the new event focused on an exchange of ideas between filmmakers 'working now, in different countries […] facing common problems' (EIFF Brochure 1979: 8).[37] Forsyth Hardy put considerable energy into a retrospective to mark the fiftieth anniversary of the Documentary Movement, which turned out to be a highly successful event (EIFF Executive Committee Minutes, 12 October 1979), albeit one that was to attract a complaint in the theoretical journal *Framework* of 'the manoeuvring into positions of power and influence of a latter-day Grierson gang' (Rodrigues 1980: 46).

The 1980 Festival marked Myles' departure to take up a post at the Pacific Film Archive in California (F. Hardy 1992: 143). Her valedictory programme, including a selection of 'personal highlights' taken from her 13-year association with EIFF,[38] reflects the lack of a clear critical stance for the Festival. A programme of early talkies from the National Film Archive, for example, was chosen 'for no other reason than that it provides an opportunity to screen some rarely seen period pieces' (EIFF Brochure 1980: 8). Five open discussions were scheduled, considering 'strategies of narration' and 'aspects of cinema as an ideological-economic institution' (EIFF Brochure 1980: 6), but there was no supporting publication and only minimal information available in the brochure. The brief renaissance in British production had been curtailed by recession (Perry 1980/81: 28) so the programme lacked the indigenous concentration of the 1979 edition. Only Paul Willemen's essay accompanying that year's Joseph H. Lewis retrospective sought to redefine the Festival's stance in relation to film culture (Willemen 1980). The Festival staff published the essay in pamphlet form, rather than in the official catalogue, suggesting an uneasy relationship with Willemen's thesis.[39] Indeed its publication caused a heated exchange at Myles' final Executive Committee meeting. Forsyth Hardy made clear that he had taken great exception to Willemen's assessment of the Festival's first 20 years as 'rigidly dogmatic' and 'relentlessly puritanical' (Willemen 1980: 1). He had countered with a scathing review of the open discussions in *The Scotsman*, a move that embarrassed other members of the committee and demoralised the festival staff (EIFF Executive Committee Minutes, 10 September 1980). Willemen's essay examines the contradictions inherent in the clash between cinéphilia and theory in the context of EIFF's programming. He does not argue for the endowment of auteur-status on Joseph H. Lewis; indeed he declares that all attempts to do so have failed. Instead, he uses the Lewis retrospective to construct a narrative discourse around the Festival itself. Willemen, who had collaborated with Myles on almost every retrospective since 1970, charts what he sees as the three stages of EIFF's development with the Lewis retrospective marking a transition towards an as yet undefined fourth period. I described Willemen's three stages in the second chapter; in this respect his argument echoes the introduction to the *Edinburgh '76* manifesto, which he had co-written with Phil Hardy and Claire Johnston.

Turning to Lewis, Willemen argues that by staging a retrospective of a filmmaker whose work resists the auteurist approach, the Festival is shaking off any 'secondary elaboration' or 'social justification for indulging in the pleasure of the look' (1980: 3). Willemen suggests that the Festival is re-introducing a de-politicised a-social cinéphilia, a 'secretive activity for initiates only'. He argues that whilst auteur theory proposed that unconscious signifiers of cinéphiliac desire are inscribed into a text as fissures 'within a coherence', Lewis's films are 'cobbled together to present the fissures. Marks of cinematic desire are presented as such, divested from any pretence of rational coherence.' To watch a Lewis film is to openly declare one's previously furtive desire for cinema; it is an experience 'verging on the pornographic'. As he declares that 1968 saw the end of cinéphilia 'except as a deliberately reactionary form of ostrich politics' (Ibid.), it is difficult to read this analysis of the Festival positively.

Explaining the essay to a partly hostile Executive Committee, Myles described it as a response to international concern that 'Edinburgh was reverting to auteurism' (Executive Committee Minutes, 10 September 1980). The Joseph H. Lewis retrospective was therefore, like the 1974 Raoul Walsh retrospective, a tool to examine structures of meaning, but at the same time an acknowledgement that such work had come adrift from any clear sense of political engagement.

Willemen has since suggested that during the 1970s British cinéphiles employed theory as an 'alibi' for their furtive desire (1994: 223). Psychoanalytic theory renamed cinéphilia as voyeurism or fetishism; the desire for cinema was considered a 'manipulation of regressive fantasies and the place of the big male escape from sexual difference' (Elsaesser 2005b: 32). There was a tendency amongst the *Screen* theorists of the time to privilege the consideration of filmic texts as a form of ideological oppression. As Elsaesser puts it, they equated illusion, or suspension of belief, with delusion, a spell from which we must be freed (2005b: 35). Willemen's 1980 pamphlet can be read as an attempt to negotiate this problem of desire versus political engagement. He implies the same of Myles herself, describing her reign as 'dependent on the tolerance of the very representatives of the film culture the festival opposed':

> Only a courageous festival director with the qualities of
> a cinéphiliac schizophrenic would attempt to hold such
> contradictions while at the same time actively encouraging the
> kind of work that could only make the job of festival director
> more difficult: the more successful the critical policy became, the
> more virulently the establishment's mouthpieces attacked it and
> clamoured for the theoretical-cultural work to be repudiated. In
> spite of such intense pressures to philistinize the Festival, Lynda
> Myles managed to retain and develop a critical policy which
> succeeded in making the festival a unique rallying point for
> progressive forces in British film culture. (Willemen 1980: 2)

Forsyth Hardy did not understand these 'intense pressures to philistinize'
(EIFF Executive Committee Minutes, 10 September 1980) and continued
to muse about what they might be in his 1992 account. Quoting an article
in a similar vein by *The Scotsman* critic Julie Davidson, he questions the
notion that Myles' project was 'reviled' by the British film establishment
(F. Hardy 1992: 143). Perhaps more revealingly, Myles herself cannot now
identify any such hostility. She acknowledges the support of the liberal
press and claims she had developed great relations with the studios and
distributors and strong friendships with 'those people who were about
to take over the industry'. Only very rarely did anyone refuse her a film.
She had also formed links with key individuals at the BFI, the BBC, the
Arts Council and the British Council and argues that without the support
of the establishment, she 'wouldn't have been able to keep going' (Myles,
Interview).

Willemen may have been over-stating the case in the highly charged
theoretical language of the time. Put in the less inflammatory words of
EIFF chairman Colin Young, both Grigor and Myles went against the
grain of the 'tremendous tendency in Scotland to be respectable',[40] in
order to 'draw attention to the fact that respectability sets an agenda that
is not necessarily the most interesting one' (Young, Interview). Taken

together, the assessments of Myles, Willemen and Young suggest that the only significant 'pressures to philistinize' came from within the Festival organisation itself. However, to simply read the actions of Forsyth Hardy and other members of the Executive Committee as philistine is both to dismiss their contribution to the radical origins of the Festival and to discount hard economic realities. Myles' tenure saw a tenfold increase in budget and by 1980 the Festival had a substantial deficit (McArthur 1990: 102). That the Executive Committee was nonetheless able to raise funds for a new centre for film exhibition in Edinburgh during this period is an indication of the Festival's new national standing. With the new Filmhouse came new responsibilities and financial commitments, commitments which paradoxically prevented the Festival from continuing the oppositional project that had transformed its reputation during the preceding decade.

It is difficult to quantify the impact of the critical discourse generated by EIFF during the period, in terms of its cultural value on the festival circuit, or in the wider culture. Reflecting on the period, Myles has remarked that 'it's very difficult to define exactly Edinburgh's contribution [to the wider application of theoretical work], but whatever we did had a kind of ripple effect' (Perry 1980/81: 28). Forsyth Hardy's account reduces the radical period to a couple of years supposedly dominated by theory (Hardy, Interview). Indeed in his 1992 history, he is able to see 'continuity and fulfilment' of the Festival's original aims throughout its (then) 45-year history, arguing that the Festival has always served 'the cinema and the community in a way the Film Guild pioneers had dreamt of' (Hardy 1992: 137). The final chapter of this account considers the period in the light of subsequent developments of the film festival phenomenon, raising the question of whether the cost of keeping EIFF alive now is the loss of any sustained critical focus beyond merely 'serving the cinema and the community'.

# Conclusion: Utopian Anomaly?

The 1980s were to herald a third stage of film festival evolution in which the rapid global spread of festivals led to increased competition and expanding audiences (de Valck 2007: 20). De Valck argues that this period saw growing homogeneity of both festival format and programming and that a neo-colonial 'dogma of discovery' generated by festivals competing to find the next 'new wave' of international cinema resulted in many filmmakers consciously creating work for an international (Western) audience, and consequently losing 'part of the original, local relevance' that made aesthetic or political new waves distinct (2007: 175-9). The simultaneous rise of domestic entertainment technology led to greater availability of world cinema through other means. In this context, which continues today, far fewer forms of cultural value generated by individual festivals are recognised as indispensable to the network. The success of each event depends largely on the freshness of its premières, and on the talent – stars, directors – attending, which in turn is dictated by marketing strategies and the specific benefits of press and industry exposure that each festival can offer.

Ken Wlaschin, director of the London Film Festival in 1981, suggested that whilst LFF 'has been structured to promote film-makers', the EIFF 'has been structured to promote film critics' (Auty et al. 1981: 13). Both Grigor and Myles are able to offer specific examples of films, neglected by their own distributors – *Easy Rider* (Dennis Hopper, U.S., 1969), *Annie Hall* (Woody Allen, U.S., 1977) – whose fortunes were transformed by a successful launch at Edinburgh. However, these anecdotes also indicate that Edinburgh's achievement in this regard was rare. Rather than sustaining a uniform policy of filmmaker promotion, Edinburgh's relative strength was in its championing of those filmmakers who were neglected elsewhere. As Myles put it at the end of her period of tenure, 'I cannot see the point in showing films that are guaranteed a release and a reasonable audience already, at least not as a general rule. It's the independents and the mavericks that we can do most to help' (quoted in Perry 1980/81: 28).

The next EIFF Artistic Director Jim Hickey (1981-88), who in his first year faced a budget slashed by more than half (F. Hardy 1992: 147), could not afford the costs involved in attracting talent and instead appealed to audiences by reaffirming 'the unrivalled experience of viewing films in cinemas' (EIFF Brochure 2006: 14). He achieved this by staging a series of unique screenings such as the recently restored five-hour silent epic *Napoléon* (Abel Gance, France, 1927), with live orchestral accompaniment in the 3,000-seat Playhouse theatre. This emphasis on spectacle can be seen as a continuation by other means of a policy of non-reliance on the international distribution network and a refusal to limit the Festival's identity to the promotion of the annual crop of new international works available, regardless of their quality relative to that of the previous or subsequent years' output.

With the rise of what de Valck identifies as contemporary cinéphilia – the commodification of film history through DVDs, theatrical re-releases and on-line journals (2007: 183) – there is arguably no place for a Festival that would, for example, screen *Jeanne Dielman, 23 Quai de Commerce – 1080 Bruxelles* (Chantal Akerman, Belgium/France, 1975) three times in five years in order to illustrate specific conference discussions.[41] Further research is required into EIFF's subsequent history, particularly the Festival's relationship with Filmhouse. However, it is possible to see in the EIFF programming of the 1970s the seeds of Filmhouse's rich year round repertory programming, which in turn has put greater pressure on the Festival to deliver the very latest films.

Former EIFF director Shane Danielsen (2002-06) has described the international festival situation in the first decade of the twenty-first century as analogous to that of the early 1960s. Programmers promote and fight over the same few prestigious art house directors whilst ignoring the commercial product playing to indigenous audiences, with the result that local film cultures are entirely misrepresented on the international circuit (Danielsen 2008: 30). Such an analysis would appear to pave the way for a reprise of the late-1960s revolution in programming, searching beyond the films that pander to international tastes, to unearth the commercial productions that truly represent the tastes of local audiences. Or is this merely to adhere to the 'dogma of discovery' (de Valck 2007), unrealistically hoping that there are still indigenous cinemas untouched by international trends and tastes, waiting to be discovered and paraded before bourgeois Western audiences like the exotic artefacts of a Victorian imperialist exhibition?

In receiving £1.88 million of Lottery funding over three years, in March 2008 EIFF was given a brief by the UK Film Council to 'massively expand its activities and profile on the world stage.' The Festival responded by moving out of the shadow of the Edinburgh International Festival to a new date in June and by formalising its interest in new talent, proclaiming its vision 'to become the world's greatest film festival of discovery' (EIFF Brochure 2008: 7). The Under the Radar strand was introduced to showcase risk-taking low-budget works by first time feature filmmakers and the Trailblazers talent development pool, instigated the previous year, was expanded. The 'dogma of discovery' that de Valck talks about inevitably puts an enormous pressure on EIFF to annually deliver the goods. It is difficult to see how adopting the template of a high profile event like Sundance can prove sustainable in a highly competitive market, particularly now that the UK Film Council's grant has come to an end.

Perhaps, therefore, an approach not dissimilar from the Ballerina Ballroom Cinema of Dreams model would be the radical option; the Festival could shift its focus away from new work, instead generating new cultural value for forgotten, neglected or over-familiar films via the context in which they are presented. Such an approach would surely demand the reinvention of the very format of the Festival in order to attract what Murray Grigor called 'writeability'. It seems that as arts funding streams across the UK dry up, are dammed or diverted, EIFF finds itself relatively free of obligation to public funders and private sponsors. The question that EIFF must ask of itself is whether the organisation still possesses the imagination, intellectual rigour and will to go against the grain and interrogate our notions of international film culture – a will that characterised the cinéphiles that took over Edinburgh in 1968.

# Notes

[1]  Although the exact title has varied during its 64 years, for convenience I will refer to it as the Edinburgh International Film Festival, EIFF or the Festival throughout.

[2]  One of the key participants, Lynda Myles, was to co-write with Michael Pye the first work examining the radical change undergone in Hollywood at this time, *The Movie Brats: How the Film Generation Took Over Hollywood* (1979). I have borrowed her title in order to examine this period of the Festival's history within its cultural context.

[3]  Indeed, Hickey had served on the festival staff since 1969 and directly contributed to the agenda set during this period.

[4]  This study was written in 2008 and was subject to constraints of time and length. More recent scholarly writing on festivals is not taken into consideration here. If I return to this project at a later point, I am likely to engage in greater analysis of the various retrospectives, as well as of the Festival's programming of cinema from Africa and Asia. Jim Hickey's contribution throughout the 1970s was far greater than acknowledged here. I hope that my work paves the way for more research into this vital period in the history of EIFF.

[5]  During the 1960s, the Golden Thistle Award was presented by the Films of Scotland Committee to individuals who had made an outstanding contribution to the Art of Cinema. The first jury award, introduced in 1993, was the British Screen-funded Michael Powell Award for Best New British Feature. Unusually, the jury deliberation was held in open session in its early years, although this practice appears to have died out in 2001 when funding of the award transferred to the new government agency for film, the UK Film Council. Other jury awards subsequently established include the Best British Short Film Award (introduced in 1998), the Best Documentary Award (2006), the Award for Best Performance in a British Feature Film (2007), the Best New International Feature Award and Best International Short Fiction Award

(both 2009). Other awards have been made by individual (and varying) sponsors – the New Directors Award (1999) and the Short Scottish Documentary Award (2002) – or by audience vote – the McLaren Award for New British Animation (1990) and the Audience Award (1997).

6    This freedom has naturally been curtailed since the 1980s as private sponsorship and increased state support became necessary for survival. Whilst this study does not seek to examine the current state of the Festival, it is worth acknowledging that the introduction of film market New British Expo in 1996 (renamed Film UK in 2000) and the Festival's recent acceptance of £1.88 million from the UK Film Council, not to mention the 2008 calendar shift to June which lessened the links with the International Arts Festival, have all had an impact on EIFF's identity.

7    At the suggestion of Peter Wollen, Paul Willemen was invited to co-edit the 1970 EIFF publication on Roger Corman with David Will.  He and his partner Claire Johnston continued to work with the programming team in subsequent years. Willemen contributed to the Douglas Sirk book in 1972, while Johnston was one of the organisers of the Women's Film Festival in the same year. They both organised the Frank Tashlin retrospective in 1973 and co-edited the accompanying book and similarly organised and co-edited the book accompanying the Jacques Tourneur retrospective in 1975 (Will, Interview).

8    Presided over by Henri Langlois, the Cinémathèque Française was an internationally renowned archive and film theatre. Langlois began collecting films at a time when it was not widely considered valuable to do so. His collection included film memorabilia and cinematographic equipment. Short of space, he famously kept film cans in his bath. Cinéma MacMahon became associated during the 1950s with a particular taste in American action pictures and with masculine stars and directors such as John Wayne, Humphrey Bogart, Raoul Walsh and Fritz Lang (Elsaesser 2005b: 27-32).

9    Nevertheless, the reinstatement of Langlois came at the formidable cost of the Cinémathèque's annual state subsidy (Harvey 1978: 15).

10  Pesaro (established in 1965) was committed to the films of Latin American directors, often banned in their own repressive states, whilst Rotterdam (established in 1972) was to focus on emerging Asian film culture (de Valck 2007: 166 and 180).

11  Formed under the influence of John Grierson, the Films of Scotland Committee was charged with promoting the life and character of Scotland through film, and was presided over by Forsyth Hardy from 1955. Established, but barely funded, by the Secretary of State for Scotland and with a staff of three, the Films of Scotland Committee sought production finance from a variety of sponsors. Hardy quickly proved himself an adept fundraiser, whilst simultaneously nurturing a new generation of filmmakers in the Griersonian tradition. See *The Films of Scotland Documentaries* website, Available HTTP: http://sites2.scran.ac.uk/films_of_scotland/index.htm ( 3 November 2008).

12  Grigor was only able achieve this last-minute coup because his fiancée's best friend was Gillo Pontecorvo's niece (Grigor, Interview).

13  After befriending them on their first visit, Langlois would ring them at their hotel every morning to give them a personally devised itinerary for the day (Myles, Interview).

14  Will formed his idea after a viewing of *Pickup on South Street* (Samuel Fuller, U.S., 1953) on late night television and as a result of Fuller's brief but memorable cameo in *Pierrot le fou* (Jean-Luc Godard, France/Italy, 1965). At that time none of his films were in theatrical circulation in the UK (Will, Interview).

15  Greeted by bagpipes at Edinburgh airport, Fuller charmed the sceptical Executive Committee with his direct, unpretentious manner, forgoing an expensive hotel suite to stay instead with Grigor, who he later described as 'like a not bad looking and kind of good looking haggard Greenwich Village fifth-rate poet […] I fell in love with the son of a bitch' (Fuller, Interview).

16  The films screened were *The Fast and the Furious* (Edward Sampson and John Ireland, U.S., 1955), *Machine-Gun Kelly* (Roger Corman, U.S., 1958),

*Out of the Darkness* (Roger Corman, U.S., 1958), *Pit and the Pendulum* (Roger Corman, U.S., 1961) and *The Little Shop of Horrors* (Roger Corman, U.S., 1960).

[17] The tribute consisted of four Fritz Lang films – *The Return of Frank James* (U.S., 1940), *Man Hunt* (U.S., 1941), *Western Union* (U.S., 1941) and *American Guerrilla in the Philippines* (U.S., 1950) – and six John Ford films – *Drums Along the Mohawk* (U.S., 1939), *Young Mr. Lincoln* (U.S., 1939), *The Grapes of Wrath* (U.S., 1940), *How Green Was My Valley* (U.S., 1941), *Tobacco Road* (U.S., 1941) and *My Darling Clementine* (U.S., 1946).

[18] The Corman films screened were *Bloody Mama* (U.S., 1970) and *Gas – Or – It Became Necessary to Destroy the World in Order to Save It* (U.S., 1970).

[19] The Fisher films screened were *Dracula* (UK, 1958), *The Brides of Dracula* (UK, 1960) and *Dracula Prince of Darkness* (UK, 1965).

[20] Geoffrey Nowell-Smith has covered this crisis in depth (2006); of importance to this account is the resulting split of SEFT from the BFI. Whilst the BFI did not wish to actively engage with the universities itself, or adopt a politicised film study culture, it did at least acknowledge the need for a new educational policy by awarding SEFT a considerable annual grant (MacCabe 1985: 6).

[21] The programme included retrospectives of Bernardo Bertolucci, Norman McLaren and Peter Watkins. There were markedly few American films, the most significant being *THX 1138* (George Lucas, U.S., 1971). The Festival had screened the student short on which the feature was based, *THX 1138 4EB* (George Lucas, U.S., 1967) three years earlier when Grigor invited Herb Kosower, director of animation at the University of Southern California, to show a selection of his students' work (Grigor, Interview).

[22] Lynda Myles remembers joking at the time that Colin MacCabe and Stephen Heath had 'only seen about five movies' (Myles, Interview). Indeed, MacCabe has since admitted that on attending the shooting of Godard's *Sauve qui peut (la vie)* (*Slow Motion*, France / West Germany / Switzerland / Austria, 1980), he realised how little he knew of filmmaking and resolved that he 'would write nothing more about the

cinema […] until [he] understood much better the whole dynamic of the production process' (1999: 13).

23  *Screen*, 12:2 (Summer 1971) had been devoted entirely to Douglas Sirk's work.

24  The First International Festival of Women's Films took place in New York in June 1972. SEFT published a collection of essays edited by Claire Johnston to accompany a similar event in London the following year in which she outlined her objections to the New York event in terms of its application of theory (Johnston 1973).

25  The programme included classic European and Hollywood titles – *Mädchen in Uniform* (Leontine Sagan, Germany, 1931), *Das Blaue Licht* (*The Blue Light*, Leni Riefenstahl, Germany, 1932) and *Dance, Girl, Dance* (Dorothy Arzner, U.S., 1940) – alongside recent fiction, avant-garde and workshop productions – *Zur Sache, Schätzchen* (*Come to the Point, Baby*, May Spils, West Germany, 1968), *La Fiancée du pirate* (*Dirty Mary / A Very Curious Girl*, Nelly Kaplan, France, 1969), *Sziget a szárazföldön* (*The Lady From Constantinople*, Judit Elek, Hungary, 1969), *Reason Over Passion* (Joyce Wieland, Canada, 1969), *Coming Attractions* (Beverly Grant Conrad, U.S., 1970), *Faustine et le bel été* (*Faustine and the Beautiful Summer*, Nina Companéez, France, 1972), *Marja pieni!* (*Little Marja / Poor Little Maria*, Elija-Elina Bergholm, Finland, 1972) and *The Other Side of the Underneath* (Jane Arden, UK, 1972).

26  David Will's formal role at the Festival ended after the 1972 event when he embarked on full-time training as a psychiatrist. He continued to contribute informally until his relationship with Lynda Myles ended early in 1975 (Myles, Interview).

27  The EIFF programme for 1973 reflected the interests of these festivals. Alongside retrospectives of American directors Frank Tashlin and Irvin Kershner, the programme made its first significant foray into the cinema of non-Western cultures with a Willemen-curated programme of popular Japanese cinema and a focus on the Senegalese director Ousmane Sembene.

28  These conferences were not as groundbreaking as the 1972 Women's Event, as SEFT had already organised weekend schools in London around the conference subjects. However, a week-long festival event was able to cater for a significantly larger (and geographically more diverse) audience. The Festival was also in a position to provide significant resources – international speakers and screenings of a wide range of features – that weekend study groups could not (Perry 1980/81: 28).

29  Films screened at the Brecht event included *Die 3 Groschen-Oper (The Threepenny Opera*, Georg Wilhelm Pabst, Germany, 1931), *Kuhle Wampe oder: Wem gehört die Welt?* (*Kuhle Wampe*, Slatan Dudow, Germany, 1932), *Hangmen Also Die* (Fritz Lang, U.S., 1943), *Geschichtsunterricht* (*History Lessons*, Jean-Marie Straub and Danièle Huillet, West Germany / Italy, 1972), *Tout Va Bien* (Jean-Luc Godard and Jean Pierre Gorin, France / Italy, 1972) and *O Lucky Man!* (Lindsay Anderson, UK, 1973).

30  Films screened at the Psychoanalysis event included *Sylvia Scarlett* (George Cukor, U.S., 1935), *Letter from an Unknown Woman* (Max Ophüls, U.S., 1948), *The Cobweb* (Vincente Minnelli, U.S., 1955), *The Birds* (Alfred Hitchcock, U.S., 1963), *Tom, Tom, The Piper's Son* (Ken Jacobs, U.S., 1969) and *Jeanne Dielman, 23 Quai de Commerce, 1080 Bruxelles* (Chantal Akerman, Belgium / France, 1975).

31  It is possible to read this last point as a snub to Forsyth Hardy, whose complaints concerning 'the Festival's preoccupation with American B movies' were a regular feature of Executive Committee meetings throughout the decade (EIFF Executive Committee Minutes, 1972-79).

32  Films screened to accompany the three strands of the History / Production / Memory event included a programme of films made by the GPO Film Unit between 1935 and 1937 by John Grierson, Len Lye and Norman McLaren, *Velikiy put* (*The Great Way*, Esfir Schub, USSR, 1927), *Chelovek s kino-apparatom* (*Man with a Movie Camera*, Dziga Vertov, USSR, 1929), *It Always Rains on Sunday* (Robert Hamer, UK, 1947) and *The Loves of Joanna Godden* (Charles Frend, UK, 1947). Also related to the event were several film and television works exploring themes of

historical representation, including *Moi, Pierre Rivière, ayant égorgé ma mère, ma soeur et mon frère...* (*Moi, Pierre Rivière*, René Allio, France, 1976), *Days of Hope* (Ken Loach, UK, 1975) and *Guerres civiles en France* (Vincent Norden, François Barat and Joël Fargas, France, 1977).

33  The other Vertov films screened were *Odinnadtsatyy* (*The Eleventh Hour*, USSR, 1928), *Entuziazm: Simfoniya Donbassa* (*Enthusiasm*, USSR, 1931) and *Tri pesni o Lenine* (*Three Songs of Lenin*, USSR, 1934).

34  MacCabe describes how *Screen* also reached an impasse in terms of its application of Althusserian Marxism. Althusser's work 'provided the intellectual space in which a specific analysis of a cultural form, in this case film and cinema, could be carried out in the conviction that, at a later date, this specificity could be related to the fundamental divisions of capital and labour and the ideological formations which played their part in the reproduction of that division'. During the 1970s this position was gradually discredited, causing internal struggles over how *Screen* could or should continue to engage with politics (MacCabe 1985: 13).

35  EIFF launched an annual Television Festival in 1976. The 1970s had, in Myles' view, seen a vacuum in British film production, whilst several of the best British directors were working in television. Contractually, work by the likes of Ken Loach couldn't be screened at a Film Festival, so the Television Festival was created in part to showcase such work (Myles, Interview).

36  The feature-length British films screened were *Alien* (Ridley Scott, U.S./UK, 1979), *Black Jack* (Ken Loach, UK, 1979), *City Farm* (Robert Smith and John Davies, UK, 1979), *The Death of Heroes* (Ian Owles and Joi Leatherbarrow, UK, 1979), *Quadrophenia* (Franc Roddam, UK, 1979), *Radio On* (Chris Petit, UK/West Germany, 1979), *Scum* (Alan Clarke, UK, 1979), *The Tempest* (Derek Jarman, UK, 1979) and *That Sinking Feeling* (Bill Forsyth, UK, 1979).

37  Significantly, the films chosen to accompany the Feminism and Cinema event are not labelled as such in the Festival brochure, whilst those titles in other themed sections are (those sections being Documentary 50, Philippine Cinema of the Seventies and A Tribute to Nicholas Ray).

This may have been a deliberate decision to avoid ghettoising female directors in the programme, but I have been unable to verify this supposition. Films by female directors screened at the 1979 Festival included *De cierta manera* (*In a Certain Way*, Sara Gómez, Julio García Espinosa, Thomas González Pérez and Tomás Gutiérrez Alea, Cuba, 1977), *Old Boyfriends* (Joan Tewkesbury, U.S., 1978), *Die Macht der Männer ist die Geduld der Frauen* (*The Power of Men Is the Patience of Women*, Cristina Perincioli, West Germany, 1978), *Vinterbørn* (*Winter-Born*, Astrid Henning-Jensen, Denmark, 1978), *Servantes du bon Dieu* (*The Handmaidens of God*, Diane Létourneau, Canada, 1979) and four films by Chantal Akerman, *Je, tu, il, elle* (*I, You, He, She*, France/Belgium, 1974), *Jeanne Dielman, 23 Quai du Commerce, 1080 Bruxelles, News From Home* (Belgium/France/West Germany, 1977) and *Les Rendezvous d'Anna* (*Anna's Meetings*, Belgium/France/West Germany, 1978).

[38] The films chosen were *Der amerikanische Freund* (*The American Friend,* Wim Wenders, West Germany/France, 1977), *Dance, Girl, Dance* (Dorothy Arzner, U.S., 1940), *Imitation of Life* (Douglas Sirk, U.S., 1959), *Mean Streets* (Martin Scorsese, U.S., 1973), *Pickup on South Street* (Samuel Fuller, U.S., 1953) and *Radio On* (Chris Petit, UK/West Germany, 1979).

[39] Willemen's essay was submitted whilst Myles was out of the country. After consultation with the Chairman, assistant director Jim Hickey made the decision to publish it separately 'because it had been aimed at a specialist (if minority) audience for whom its contents would be perfectly meaningful and comprehensible' (EIFF Executive Committee Minutes, 10 September 1980). This explanation seems incomplete at best considering that Willemen's introductory texts to successive retrospectives, using similarly 'specialist' language, had until now been published in the main souvenir brochure.

[40] Murray Grigor remembers smuggling Andy Warhol's *Flesh* (Paul Morrissey, U.S., 1968) through customs in Films of Scotland cans (Grigor, Interview).

[41] The film was screened in 1975, at the Psychoanalysis event in 1976, and at the Feminism and Cinema event in 1979.

# Works Cited

(NLS = National Library of Scotland, Edinburgh)

Auty, Martyn and Gillian Hartnoll (eds) (1981) *Water Under the Bridge: 25 Years of the London Film Festival*. London: BFI.

Brewster, Ben (ed.) (1975) 'Brecht Event', *Screen,* 16:4 (Winter), 3-118.

Caughie, John (1977/78) 'The Television Event', *Screen*, 18:4 (Winter), 91-107.

——— (ed.) (1981) *Theories of Authorship*. New York: Routledge/Keegan and Paul.

Corless, Kieron and Chris Darke (2007) *Cannes: Inside the World's Premier Film Festival*. London: Faber & Faber.

Danielsen, Shane (2008) 'Cinema of the New Europe: Out of the Past', *Sight and Sound*, 18:6 (June), 26-31.

De Valck, Marijke (2007) *Film Festivals: From European Geopolitics to Global Cinéphilia*. Amsterdam: Amsterdam University Press.

Dupin, Christophe (2006) 'The Postwar Transformation of the British Film Institute and Its Impact on the Development of a National Film Culture in Britain', *Screen*, 47:4 (Winter), 443-51.

*Edinburgh International Film Festival Brochures 1947-2008*. Edinburgh: Edinburgh International Film Festival.

*Edinburgh International Film Festival Director's Report, November 1976*, NLS: Acc.11308, MS. 7.

*Edinburgh International Film Festival Executive Committee Minutes*, 9 September 1967-10 September 1980, NLS: Acc.11308, MSS. 5-8.

Elsaesser, Thomas (2005a) *European Cinema: Face to Face with Hollywood*. Amsterdam: Amsterdam University Press.

——— (2005b) 'Cinéphilia or the Uses of Disenchantment' in Marijke de Valck and Malte Hagener (eds) *Cinéphilia: Movies, Love and Memory*. Amsterdam: Amsterdam University Press, 27-44.

Garnham, Nicholas (1971) *Samuel Fuller*. London: Secker and Warburg for the BFI.

Hardy, Forsyth (1950) 'The Edinburgh Film Festival', *Hollywood Quarterly*, 5:1 (Autumn), 33-40.

—— (1976) 'Notes on Agenda for Executive Committee Meeting 26th November', 3 November 1976, NLS: Acc.11308, MS.7.

—— (1992) *Slightly Mad and Full of Dangers*. Edinburgh: Ramsey Press.

Hardy, Phil (1970) *Samuel Fuller*. London: Studio Vista.

—— (ed.) (1974) *Raoul Walsh*. Edinburgh: Edinburgh International Film Festival.

——, Claire Johnston and Paul Willemen (eds) (1976) *Edinburgh '76 Magazine*. Edinburgh: Edinburgh International Film Festival.

Harvey, Sylvia (1978) *May '68 and Film Culture*. London: BFI.

—— (1982) 'Whose Brecht? Memories for the Eighties: A Critical Recovery', *Screen*, 23:1 (May/June), 45-59.

Johnston, Claire (1973) *Notes on Women's Cinema*. London: SEFT.

—— (ed.) (1977) *Edinburgh '77 Magazine*. Edinburgh: Edinburgh International Film Festival.

Lloyd, Matthew (2008) 'How the Movie Brats Took Over Edinburgh', *The Drouth*, 28 (Summer), 61-7.

Lloyd, Matthew (2010) 'Edinburgh International Film Festival and the Dogma of Discovery', *The Drouth*, 37 (Autumn), 52-7.

MacCabe, Colin (1975) 'Walsh an Author?', *Screen*, 16:1 (Spring), 128-34.

—— (1985) 'Class of '68: Elements of an Intellectual Autobiography 1967-81', in *Theoretical Essays: Film: Literature: Linguistics*, Manchester: Manchester University Press, 1-32.

—— (1999) *The Eloquence of the Vulgar*. London: BFI.

Macpherson, Donald (1976/77) 'Edinburgh Film Festival 1976', *Screen*, 17:4 (Winter), 105-11.

McArthur, Colin (1990) 'The Rises and Falls of the Edinburgh International Film Festival', in Eddie Dick (ed.) *From Limelight to Satellite: A Scottish Film Book*. London: British Film Institute/Scottish Film Council, 91-102.

Mulvey, Laura (1975) 'Visual Pleasure and Narrative Cinema', *Screen*, 16:3 (Autumn), 6-18.

Munro, Emily (2006) *The Language Problem in European Cinema. Discourses on 'Foreign-Language Films' in Criticism, Theory and Practice.* Glasgow: University of Glasgow. Unpublished PhD Thesis.

Myles, Lynda (1977a) 'Toronto: The Festival of Festivals, October 13th-24th 1976', (February), NLS: Acc.11308, MS.7.

—— (1977b) 'Policy Statement Edinburgh International Film Festival', (April), NLS: Acc.11308, MS.7.

—— and Michael Pye (1979) *The Movie Brats: How the Film Generation Took Over Hollywood.* London: Faber & Faber.

Nash, Mark and Steve Neale (1977/78) 'Film History/Production/Memory', *Screen*, 18:4 (Winter), 77-91.

Nichols, Bill (1994) 'Discovering Form, Inferring Meaning: New Cinemas and the Film Festival Circuit', *Film Quarterly*, 47:3 (Spring), 16-30.

Nowell-Smith, Geoffrey (2006) 'The 1970 Crisis at the BFI and Its Aftermath', *Screen*, 47:4 (Winter), 453-9.

Perry, Simon (1980/81) 'An Edinburgh Woman: Simon Perry Interviews Lynda Myles', *Sight and Sound*, 50:1 (Winter), 27-8.

Rodrigues, Chris (1980) 'Edinburgh', *Framework*, 13 (Autumn), 46-7.

Sarris, Andrew (1979) 'Notes on the Auteur Theory in 1962', in Gerald Mast and Marshall Cohen (eds) *Film Theory and Criticism.* New York: Oxford University Press, 650-65.

*Screen*, 12:2 (Summer 1971). Special issue on Douglas Sirk.

*Screen*, 15:2 (Summer 1974). Special issue on Brecht and a Revolutionary Cinema.

Selfe, Melanie (2007) 'Doing the Work of the NFT in Nottingham – or How to Use the BFI to Beat the Communist Threat in Your Local Film Society', *Journal of British Cinema and Television*, 4:1, 80-100.

—— (forthcoming) 'The View From Outside London' in Geoffrey Nowell-Smith and Christophe Dupin (eds) *The British Film Institute: The Government and Film Culture 1933-2007.* Manchester: Manchester University Press.

Stanfield, Peter (2008) 'Notes Toward a History of the Edinburgh International Film Festival, 1969-77', *Film International*, 6:4, 63-71.

Stanford, Lynne (2006) *The Changing Faces of Edinburgh's International Film Festival: The Lynda Myles Years (1969-1977)*. Edinburgh: University of Edinburgh, Unpublished MSc Dissertation.

Stringer, Julian (2001) 'Global Cities and the International Film Festival Economy', in Mark Shiel and Tony Fitzmaurice (eds) *Cinema and the City: Film and Urban Societies in a Global Context*. London: Blackwell, 134-44.

—— (2003) 'Raiding the Archive: Film Festivals and the Revival of Classic Hollywood', in Paul Grainge (ed.) *Memory and Popular Film*. Manchester: Manchester University Press, 81-96.

Turan, Kenneth (2002) *From Sundance to Sarajevo*. London: University of California Press.

UK Film Council (2008) 'Major £1.88 million Lottery cash injection for Edinburgh Film Festival', (17 March). On-line. Available HTTP: http:// www.ukfilmcouncil.org.uk/news?show=13675&page=1&step=10 (3 November 2008).

Whitaker, Sheila (1978) 'Edinburgh', *Framework*, 7/8 (Spring), 41-2.

Will, David (1967) 'Letter', *The Scotsman*, 4 September 1967, 6.

—— and Peter Wollen (eds) (1969) *Samuel Fuller*. Edinburgh: Edinburgh International Film Festival/Scottish International.

—— and Paul Willemen (eds) (1970) *Roger Corman*. Edinburgh/Cambridge: Edinburgh International Film Festival/Cinema Magazine.

Willemen, Paul (1980) 'The Edinburgh Film Festival and Joseph H. Lewis', Edinburgh International Film Festival, NLS: Acc.11308, MSS. 181.

—— (1994) 'Through the Glass Darkly: Cinéphilia Reconsidered' in *Looks and Frictions: Essays in Cultural Studies and Film Theory*. Bloomington/ London: Indiana University Press/BFI, 223-257.

Wollen, Peter (1969) *Signs and Meaning in the Cinema*. Bloomington/ London: Indiana University Press/BFI.

—— (1975) 'The Two Avant-Gardes', *Studio International*, 978 (November/ December), 171-175. On-line. Available HTTP: http://www. medienkunstnetz.de/source-text/100/ (3 November 2008).

—— (1981) 'The Avant-Gardes: Europe and America', *Framework*, 14 (Spring), 9-10.

# Interviews Cited


Anstey, Edgar, Interview Transcript, 1986. NLS: Acc.11308, MS.1201.

Fuller, Samuel, Interview Transcript, 1986. NLS: Acc.11308, MS.1201.

Grigor, Murray, Unpublished Interview by Matthew Lloyd, 29 May 2008.

Hardy, Forsyth, Interview Transcript, 1986. NLS: Acc.11308, MS.1201.

Malcolm, Derek, Interview Transcript, 1986. NLS: Acc.11308, MS.1201.

Mulvey, Laura, Interview Transcript, 1986. NLS: Acc.11308, MS.1201.

Myles, Lynda, Unpublished Interview by Matthew Lloyd, 20 June 2008.

Will, David, Unpublished Interview by Matthew Lloyd, 7 July 2008.

Young, Colin, Interview Transcript, 1986. NLS: Acc.11308, MS.1201.

# About the Author

Matthew Lloyd is a filmmaker, curator and festival producer. He worked for the Edinburgh International Film Festival for 10 years, as both a programmer and an administrator. Matthew has produced two high profile film events for Tilda Swinton and Mark Cousins, the *Ballerina Ballroom Cinema of Dreams* in 2008 and *A Pilgrimage* in 2009. Now based in Glasgow, he programmes shorts for *The Magic Lantern* and the *Glasgow Short Film Festival*. Matthew has also directed three short films, which have screened at various international festivals.